RECLAIMED!

RECLAIMED!

The story of
GEORGE and SUE HAYES

Written by Helen Penfold

TORBAY PUBLISHING
PAIGNTON, DEVON

Editorial, design and typesetting by
Nuprint Services Ltd, Harpenden, Herts.

Printed in England for
TORBAY PUBLISHING LTD
Preston, Paignton, Devon TQ3 1JP
by Cox & Wyman, Reading.

Contents

Thanks

The first person we need to thank is the Lord, for without His guidance and help, nothing would have been achieved. There have been many who have given information and we are grateful to all of them. Our particular thanks go to Helen Penfold whose perseverance and enthusiasm have helped us; amazingly enough, we have still remained friends.

Lesley Harwood has also given advice and helpful comments and Janet Clark typed her way laboriously through the manuscript. Our cat had to listen to it all so we must show our appreciation to her.

May the Lord take and use this book to His glory and honour.

George and Sue Hayes

Foreword

It is a privilege to write the foreword to this book and I do so with pleasure. I am reminded of a story told about Oliver Cromwell when an artist wanted to paint his portrait with a view to flattering him. The Lord Protector said, 'I want it painted just as it is – warts and all!' This book has not been written to flatter, and the story has been told simply – 'just as it is'.

Here we have a couple of 'rough diamonds' being cut and polished by a master craftsman – at times feeling the pain involved in the process – but conscious of the fact that all the time they are being conformed to the likeness of God's Son. Helen has written in the first person, which helps to bring out their personal testimony to what God has done and is doing in their lives.

This book also reflects the church fellowship through which George and Sue have been helped and nurtured — not a perfect church by any means — but one which is struggling to become what God wants it to be.

I pray that this book will be used to bring many people to trust in Jesus Christ as their personal

Saviour and Lord, and also to encourage others who have made this commitment of their lives to go on 'being transformed into His likeness with ever increasing glory'.

Rev. Reg Bottoms

PART ONE

LIFE
IN THE
BALANCE

1   *Death closes my door*

Sue's story...

As my life hung in the balance it suddenly seemed very precious.

'The operation is over – just lie there quietly,' a voice whispered close to my ear. A dull pain filled me and I shut my eyes and drifted in a land halfway between sleeping and waking. It was enough to be alive! My life flashed before me and I thought of the days when Beatlemania was sweeping the country and Cliff Richard dominated the hit parade. I remembered the day I went to visit my mother.

I was thinking that this wasn't like a hospital, there was no smell of antiseptic hanging in the air, as I made my way from the road to the heavy wooden front door. Dad walked beside me, his eyes, though tired, were clear and bright. His tanned face and broad forehead were wrinkled slightly. Black thinning hair had been carefully combed into place.

'Well, Susan, today has come at last, I hope Mum's ready for us,' he smiled at me.

Rather nervously I felt the clip which held my long black hair tightly behind my back and breathed a sigh of satisfaction. It was still neatly tied. Mum had left home when I was a child, but now I was emerging as a woman. Two men shuffled past us and stared blankly in front of them. I felt a touch of pity and a slight feeling of fear as I stood waiting with Dad in the entrance hall. A tall, muscular man in an overall came towards us and spoke.

'Mr Byrne, your wife will be here in a minute. You can wait in the TV lounge over there.'

Silently, we went into the room and took seats near the window. The sunlight streaked across the coffee table. There were five or six people near us. A girl who looked about fourteen was watching the television. There didn't look much wrong with her. An old lady, who was knitting, sat in the corner opposite us. The clock on the wall ticked ominously. I picked up a magazine and flicked through the pages, hardly reading it. Dad puffed at a cigarette. Mum appeared about a quarter of an hour later in the doorway. Her white hair made her look a striking figure. She was slim and rather distinguished; her face had the slight tense expression that I never saw her without.

'Ernest, my case is packed, we can go now.' Without saying anything to me she went over to a middle-aged lady who was sitting with a young boy. 'I'll be back to visit you before long, Ethel. Don't eat too much will you?' Mum was smiling gently at her.

'Look after yourself, Queenie. I hope not to see you in here again as a patient,' Ethel remarked placidly. She stood up and clasped my mother in rather a plump embrace.

Dad took my mother's arm and moved her firmly towards the door. I followed behind my parents and at last Mum spoke to me as we stood waiting at the bus stop.

'Well, Susan, how are you and your brothers? You're leaving school, Dad says.'

'Tony and Paul are forever messing about with their car as usual. And I think I've got a job!' It was a pleasure to talk freely to my mother and a rare experience. I chatted as we got on the bus. We passed the ruins at Avebury but I hardly noticed the countryside.

We'd tidied up at home quickly before Mum came back, but I knew what she was thinking as she stepped over the threshold of our terraced house.

'You've certainly let this place go. I'll have to sort it out. Let's have a coffee,' she said, as Dad closed the front door.

Dad then lugged her case up the narrow stairs. The case bumped against the side of the wall as he went up. I made the coffee. Mum was sitting on a stool and seemed happier than I had known her before. We were now a complete family. Mum was a stranger to me; Dad was the real figure in my life. He fed me, laughed with me and wiped away my tears. He was the centre of my life. Mum was rather quiet, but I guessed it was the tablets. We all sat around drinking coffee. As soon as I had finished, Mum whisked the coffee cups away and then washed them up. Soon she was scrubbing away at the kitchen sink. 'Some things never change,' I thought. Mum was the most houseproud person I have ever met.

Sarah called for me the following evening and we went out for coffee at the local café. She was the best friend I had. Other girls didn't like me much, as they felt I was after their boyfriends. They were probably right! Sarah was plain-faced with a long Roman-shaped nose and a rather lanky figure. With her I shared all my secrets.

'How's your Mum?' she broke into my thoughts as I was playing with the sugar in the basin.

'Mum; oh, she's the best I have seen her for a long time. She's quiet though. She was up first thing this morning hoovering before I went to school.' I was feeling a bit hot in my tight black coat so I got up, slipped it off and put it on the back of the chair.

'You wouldn't catch my Mum up until I was safely out of the house in the mornings,' Sarah said and then took a bite out of her doughnut. I would have liked one but it seemed best to watch my figure.

I was a dumpy child who had always indulged in food and I didn't want to be a plump teenager. I resisted the temptation and instead watched Sarah with her skeleton figure with envy, and sighed.

'Sarah, how about coming to the pictures with me on Sunday afternoon? There's a great film on about King Kong.'

'Sorry, Sue, Sunday is out, I go to church then. That's the one time I can't make it.'

I looked down at the red gingham tablecloth and wondered how many times she'd refused me now. I added, 'I don't see why you go. Dad sent me to Sunday School when I was little. When I was ten I wriggled out of it and haven't been anywhere since.'

'I happen to like it,' Sarah smiled and her face lit up, 'You should try it sometime, you never know, you might even enjoy it!'

'That's one place you won't find me going with you, black crows standing in front of the congregation,' I shuddered slightly and got up. 'Come on, let's go and play some records at your house.' Sarah paid and we left.

Sarah didn't mention going with her again until five weeks later. By that time I had begun work in a shop and didn't like it much. I kept on asking her to go to the cinema with me as I didn't have a boyfriend at the time and so she was the obvious choice. I dreaded sitting there alone although I would have had the cheek to have picked up a boy if I could have found one. Sarah and I went to the park and sat on a bench, watching the boys going past.

'I'm sorry Sue, I can't,' she said which must have been for the twentieth time. I felt crafty and hoped my idea would work.

'Sarah, you come to the pictures with me and I'll go to church with you,' I was playing with a new ring on my finger as I looked across at her.

'As long as you come to church with me first. I'll go with you on Sunday to the pictures,' she knew she had won, as she glanced at my face, I laughed out loud,

'It's a bargain; call for me next Sunday! I promise I won't chicken out. You got me there, after all! Mind you, you have to keep your side, we go to the cinema afterwards!' Two rather attractive boys walked along just then and I openly stared at them. Boys were definitely interesting; one of them looked questioningly at me and smiled. My long hair hung loosely around my shoulders. I felt good and carefree that day.

Hanging around on Sunday morning I was bored, when suddenly my brother Tony asked me whether I wanted a ride in his old jalopy. I leapt at the chance. My brother was years older than me and I was his kid sister.

'Come on Susie, hop in and I'll take you for a spin. I've fixed the brakes so you needn't worry.'

We were open to the sky as he gathered speed and headed out of town. Exhilaration took away my boredom and although at times I shut my eyes, rather than watch the way he took the corners, I enjoyed the trip. When he pulled up outside our red-bricked terraced house, I was still glad I had gone. Paul, my other brother let us in, and remarked casually, 'Dad and Mum have already left.'

I had forgotten they were going back to visit Mum's friend in hospital. It was with a bitter feeling of disappointment that I entered the living room. Dad had left before I had kissed him goodbye. I may have been fifteen but I always kissed him when he left the house. In many ways at least for my Dad, I was just a little girl.

Tony and Paul were tinkering under the bonnet of the car in the early afternoon but they came in later. Tony sprawled himself over the sofa and Paul was lounging by the fireplace when the bell rang insistently.

'She's keen to get me to church,' I joked to Paul, inching my way out of the room and along the passage to the front door. Tony laughed and called after me,

'You know you're a sinner, Sue.' I tugged at the door handle. It opened and my mouth dropped open in dismay. A big bulky policeman stood on the door-step, a stern expression on his face.

'Is Mr Byrne junior at home?'

'I am sorry, my Dad's out. Can I help you?' I answered automatically, 'My brothers are here.'

'May I come in. I've something of a personal

nature to tell you.' He came inside and I led him into the room where my brothers were.

'Has something happened to my grandfather?' I asked.

'No, I'm afraid I have to inform you that your father is dead. He died on his way to visit Roundways Hospital. Your mother is O.K. She is resting there.'

The policeman's warm sympathy didn't evaporate any of my shock. I thought God was punishing me because I was going to church for the wrong reasons. He was getting His own back at me. He's so cruel. Why my Dad? I didn't want anything more to do with Him!

'I'm afraid you will have to go and stay with your aunt until the funeral. Your Dad is to be buried in Weston and they are taking him there.' He left and we packed up and went over to my aunt's.

That afternoon my life just disintegrated. I walked around in a dream. Tears came and went, leaving my heart hardened with a pain I couldn't share. The only time I never kissed him goodbye, and now, never to see him again. Life had been kind to me up until that point. I was reaping a harvest of grief and loneliness in that funeral week. Dad was mine and he was gone.

Mum came home. 'Dust to dust, ashes to ashes' vibrated through my thoughts. Work took my mind off things but I felt and acted like a robot. Mum obviously missed Dad and she continued obsessively cleaning the house. Tony was away working and Paul and I carried on our cat-and-dog like existence. As Mum grew worse, I worried about what would happen when she was taken into hospital. Three months later, Sarah's Mum offered me a room. Paul stayed at home and I moved in with my friend and lived there for about seven months. I got a job in a shoe shop which was better paid.

Mum came out in the August and I moved back home. Looking after her weighed heavily on me and I came in at nights to find her either washing the curtains or brushing the stairs. She never sat still and it made it difficult for me to relax.

'How was work, Sue?' she said picking up a leaf that had dropped on the carpet from her potted geranium.

'My legs are killing me, but I sold six pairs of shoes, so I suppose not too bad,' I mumbled with my mouth full of a sandwich.

'It's lonely during the day on my own,' she said sadly and quietly. Anxiously, I looked at my mother but didn't say anything. Paul got in from work and we began a slanging match.

'You look dolled up, who are you after?' he said sneeringly.

'None of your business; you live your life and I'll live mine!'

'I don't like the crowd you mix with, really common some of them look,' I swung out a fist but he ducked and laughed.

'Leave each other be,' Mum said, 'Susan, take these jeans of yours upstairs.'

Furious, I stormed upstairs and slammed the bedroom door. I was tough and able to live my own life. No one could pull a fast one on me, but my brother got under my skin. The less I saw of him the better!

The shoe shop was busy and the manager called to

me to fetch some shoes for the old lady he was attending. I climbed up and grabbed the box and promptly fell down the steps. The doctor signed me off work for a fortnight. It was painful to walk. Black and purple bruises, which gradually turned to yellow, festooned my legs. I hobbled around in the house. If I sat with a cup of coffee relaxing, Mum would swoop down and whisk it away, and if I dropped a magazine on the floor she bent down, picked it up and scolded me.

'Susan, you're so untidy, you make more work for me. As if I haven't enough to do!' Mum was getting thinner and her expression had a faintly worried look. She ran her fingers through her silvery white hair very often. I pulled out a cigarette and lit it and took a drag.

'Susan, that's a disgusting habit. It's so dirty,' Mum was on the warpath again. She handed me an ashtray the minute I sat down. I was beginning to enjoy the thought of going back to work. In my second week off work Mum began talking of suicide.

'I can't bear to be alone. I'll kill myself if you leave me here.'

'I have to go back sometime. It's only a few hours a day,' I said firmly, but Mum began weeping.

'I can't go on. You don't know what it's like for me. I don't know what to do next. I can't bear the silence.' Mum wept and I had to go to the doctor. By lunch time the following day she was in hospital and Paul and I were on our own again. This time I lived at home. We had fights every day.

'Take that muck off your face,' he moaned at me, 'I'm looking after you now.'

'Just get lost. I'm my own boss.' I shouted back at him. So it went on until I couldn't imagine life without a home battleground. We called a truce when we took the bus to see my Mum.

Thick snowdrifts had formed, but the road was clear most of the route. The bus went slowly and the journey took so long. We were dropped off outside the hospital gates. The grounds looked lovely. Snow had covered the lawns and formed blankets over the stark drabness of the leafless trees. Paul and I were met by Mum in the hallway. She wouldn't speak to us except to say, 'I don't want to see either of you again.'

Fifteen minutes later we were back at the bus stop. I had never been so hurt before. My heart was saddened and the blackness of depression held me in its grip. My mother wasn't coming home again. It meant nothing to her, but I continued visiting her the five years she lived. When she died, it was as if a link in my past had broken irretrievably. Tony and Paul did their best to comfort me, but at twenty I was definitely on my own. I was untouched by love.

2 Going to the devil

George's story...

My mate swung open the door and I followed his
bulky form into the dimly lit pub. I saw Sue sitting
with a girlfriend at the bar. She was swinging her
long legs, straight black hair hung around her
shoulders, mascara darkened her eyelashes. I wasn't
particularly interested until my mate John raised his
hand and waved at her friend, calling out, 'Hi, Jane,
what'yer drinking?'

I trailed along behind him, listening as he talked
non-stop.

'I haven't seen you lately. Introductions all round,
George, this is Jane and I'm afraid I don't know your
name? He looked enquiringly at the dark-haired girl
I had noticed.

'Me, I'm Sue and yes I'd definitely like a drink,'
she said cheekily, and moved over to let us in between
Jane and herself. I perched myself on the stool next to
her and gave her a smile. She gave me a cool calcu-
lating look and then turned away and ignored me.
What a hit I had made! John ordered beer for us and
gin and tonic for the ladies. Sue remained silent, any

lack of conversation on our part being made up for by the chatter coming from John and Jane. After a few minutes John got up and spoke to Jane.

'How about a dance?'

A small band was playing in the next room. Jane smiled up at him, 'I don't mind if I do.'

They went off and I was left with Sue!

'Have you heard the joke about the Irishman?' I remarked casually, to the slim, pretty dark-haired girl.

'No, I haven't,' she said briefly and shifted on her seat until she was looking at me. I recounted it and watched her laugh. I'd broken down her icy front. After another drink I asked her to dance, leading her into the other room where the band was playing some slow vibrating music. I put my arm around her and drew her close. It was too noisy so we danced in silence. Her head was resting against my shoulder. I drifted along with my own thoughts. It was good to be home. I had just spent a year in Aden.

As a Royal Marine who joined up at sixteen, I considered myself as a man of the world. A year in the blistering heat and the yellow desolate desert made me a man. Three weeks before I left Aden I nearly became a corpse. The regiment had been on exercise in the desert. We were travelling in a convoy of lorries. Perspiration saturated the compulsory uniform. My shirt was stuck to my back, and I was longing for a cool beer to drown my thirst. It was pure misery as the rays of the sun beat into my unprotected back. We moved along slowly. A Land Rover with two officers and three men led the team. The Land Rover drove over a land mine hidden in the sand and was blown into the sky. The sound of the explosion carried for miles across the desert wastes, two corpses were left and injured, bleeding men were lying on the sand. Travelling behind the Land Rover we had a full view. It was a horrible sight. As quickly as we could, we got the injured men to the base medical centre. The suddenness of death in the desert struck home to me. I didn't like it; the presence of death made me feel uncomfortable. I didn't need anyone to tell me it could have been me. It was a raw, rugged life in the Marines. Life was an exciting adventure; we worked hard and played hard. Arriving home in Portsmouth, I fell for a girl but she lived near another base. I schemed to get posted there. A course in cordon bleu cookery was the only way. Without ever having boiled an egg I got myself on it. The course of true love never runs smooth. I arrived and she ditched me and all I was left with was a cookery course which I couldn't drop! It was on holiday leave that I ended up in the pub, dancing with Sue.

While we danced I invited Sue through the din out for a meal. She didn't say no. John and Jane joined us. I was at my best, pulling out my stock of jokes and they all responded by laughing. It was an hilarious evening which ended at Sue's front door.

'How about seeing me for another meal?' I asked after a quick kiss. She hesitated a moment and then said, 'Why not. When?'

'Pick you up tomorrow at 8,' I said casually. And so the days passed and she became like a mate to me.

Some Argentinians took a plane hostage on the

Falkland Islands and when they were sent packing, my platoon was ordered in to keep the peace. (Though what they thought thirty-two men could do if there was a full-scale invasion, I don't know!) I was in the Falklands a year. The people were nice and I enjoyed myself, but it was a relief to get back to good old England, even if it was foggy.

I found Sue in Swindon and three months together felt like a lifetime. It was like taking a bath, getting married. We just did it. There was nothing romantic about our wedding day. Sue turned up at the registry office in a blue patterned frock with long sleeves, her hair was backcombed making her face look rounder. She had pinned a white carnation onto her coat. The legal part over, we celebrated in an Indian restaurant and together drank ourselves into a stupor. Sue and I almost rolled into bed.

In a small flat in the middle of town we began our married life. The first day of our marriage began for me at 8 o'clock with a hammering at the door. I dragged myself out of bed and struggled to the door. I felt ill. Paul (Sue's older brother) stood outside the door grinning from ear to ear.

'How would you like to earn a tenner, George? I've got a job on.'

'Wouldn't I? Just hold on a minute and I'll be with you.' I pulled a tee shirt over my tanned chest and grabbed my drainpipe trousers from where I had thrown them the night before. Sue was still sleepy and looked at me with bleery eyes.

'George, where are you going at this hour?'

'Paul's here. He wants me do a job with him. I won't be too long. After all, a tenner will come in handy.' I bent over her and gave her a kiss as she lay there. I grabbed my jacket off the peg and outside the front door I put it on. Paul and I spent the day together and the night in the pub. Long after dark I got home to a very wide-awake Sue. Her language that night rivalled my own.

Leaving the Marines was a problem I faced after my two boys were born. The parades and drill bored me. I became so restless that one day without telling anyone I upped and left. I was on the run and began living the life of a fugitive. Sue shared it with me. Walking the streets openly became impossible as I was afraid of being recognised. I changed my name. I couldn't take a regular job, but I looked for casual ones. Because it was winter when I fled, there was no work and we all went hungry. For a while Sue got some money from the social welfare but it didn't last long. Our friends used a special knock when visiting us. Otherwise we never answered the door. We were terrified of the military police.

When spring came and the trees broke into bud, things looked a bit brighter. I worked as a window cleaner and got a job as a brick-layer on a building site. We moved a little above starvation level but not much. In the jobs I got, no one asked me questions. I was always passing through. I used a false name; it suited me. The rent got paid and food reached the larder shelves. Our family life remained intact.

One morning Sue told me her secret. She was pregnant again. It gave me such a jolt I flopped into a chair.

'Are you sure, Sue?'

'Yes, I'm certain now; it'll be in about seven months.' Sue was calmness herself.

'Here am I on the run, and you're expecting,' I said exasperated.

'I can't help that, George,' she said, biting an apple, 'You know jolly well it's got to be your fault.'

I went around gloomy for a few days. Tony, Sue's older brother, decided to act. He came to see me, inviting himself over the threshold by putting his foot inside the door as soon as I opened it a crack. I couldn't help feeling on edge about visitors.

'Look, we've got to talk, George. With Sue pregnant you've got to give yourself up.'

As I looked sullenly at him he sat down on our old brown, faded sofa and continued, 'What else are you going to do, George? Spend your life on the run with a false name and always looking over your shoulder? You haven't any choice; you can't get a regular job. Think of Sue. I'll pick you up on Monday and run you to Portsmouth. You can hand yourself in then. Maybe they'll go easy with you.'

Sue jumped at the idea and with as good a grace as possible, I gave in. Tony turned up early and after a brief farewell to Sue, he drove me to the Portsmouth barracks.

I knew what I faced. The court martial took place at my old base in Kent. I was kept waiting two months for my trial and I got weekend passes home to visit Sue. The date of the hearing was set. The day before was boring. I spent my day in a stark barrack room. The sight of the major who was to defend me was welcome. We shook hands and I told him my story, all the time gaining the impression he was listening sympathetically. When I had finished, he got up saying he would try and help me. As he was leaving he said,

'By the way George, would you like to come to church with me tomorrow?' Astonished, I looked at him and mechanically said, 'I don't see why not.' With the weight of losing my freedom on my mind I spent the evening drinking myself into oblivion and surfaced the following morning with a splitting headache and feeling as if I had been run over by a London bus. I groaned as I moved off my bunk. Splashing with cold water I decided I couldn't make church. The major looked a little disappointed when I told him I felt too unwell to go.

The court hearing was in a typical military fashion and the verdict when it came was expected. Nine months sounded to me like my funeral. I began the prison sentence but immediately lodged an appeal. I wanted to be home before the baby was born. I knew a lightening of spirit when my sentence was reduced to five months. I calculated I would be home just before the baby was born. The major came in to visit me with the news. The padre also came along. The major pulled out a book with an attractive cover and handed it to me as I stood before him half at attention.

'I thought you might like something to read, George. The book's called *The Cross and the Switchblade*. It's the story of a tough guy who became a Christian. He found God was real for him. Enjoy reading it.'

'Well, thanks, I don't mind reading it; it will help pass the time in here.' I smiled. He left me alone in the small cell. I nodded at the padre who followed him out. There was nothing to do all week, so eventually sticking my feet with the shoes still on them, along the bunk, I settled myself. Propping up on an elbow I began to read, only interrupted when the sausages and mash or beans and corned beef were served up. The guards were friendly enough but the confined space got on my nerves. There wasn't much of a view from the window either. It felt like prison!

Sunday was the only day we were let out and that was for church. We were marched across to the High Anglican church just outside the perimeter gates, escorted by the guards wearing armbands. Our arms swinging in the breeze, all in rigid file as we entered the church. They made us sit in the front pews, perhaps to stop us making our escape! We were very conspicuous and a spectacle to the interested congregation who weren't that many in number. A choir sang and I didn't find it too bad when I could thumb my way expertly through the hymn book. The sermon sent me to sleep, but it wasn't a bad hour. It was a good deal worse leaving and being marched regimentally back each Sunday through the barrack gates. All we had to face then was another week locked away from the outside world.

I devoured *The Cross and the Switchblade* and played with the novel idea that God was around and had something to do with His creation. I came to the conclusion I would try and get the sequel about the guy called Nicky Cruz. Everything I tried drew a blank. Out of luck and with a finished book and endless hours of boredom I thought about Sue and the kids. She was now like a flower in full bloom. The baby was kicking within her and she was wearing bright maternity smocks. Pregnancy suited her and she was still a good looking sight to behold. It may have been her third pregnancy but it didn't show. With me inside, it was no fun for her, but at least she was getting paid regularly which was her only consolation. Her pregnancy had benefited me; it had helped reduced my sentence to only five months. At times getting out became an obsession. I wanted to get out of detention and out of the Marines *now*, as I no longer felt the same as when I joined up. Soon after the prison gates yielded, I was seeking my permanent release from the forces. Later I managed to get my discharge from the Marines and surprisingly it was an honourable one!

We now had a baby girl to join our two growing sons and now the flat was too crowded, but it wasn't much better when we moved into a rented house. I was picking up jobs locally, turning my hand to anything; unemployment wasn't a problem at that time. With a sturdy healthy frame, outside work came easily. I worked where I pleased, though we were still short of money. It was difficult for me to get a night out at the local. Window cleaning didn't bring in as much as I hoped. Being back in civvy street was teaching me what I missed, or rather, how well looked after I had been in the Royal Marines.

Leaving school at fourteen and a half and joining my uncle going around from door to door selling logs had been my only experience of regular work outside the Marines. For over ten years I had spent most of my time cushioned from the outside world. The services had given me a taste for booze, but no money limited me and I couldn't indulge in that as much as I liked. When a fourth child turned up—another boy—I had to shoulder my responsibilities. I didn't know where to get a job for life. I wasn't very satisfied at the way things were going.

I took my problems to my grandmother's funeral and surprisingly there I got the answer. My dad had been a collector of scrap metal for years. He worked with a partner who quit after I had left the Marines. Dad was ageing and he looked around him for help. He had too much work and no hands. After the funeral service was over, he approached me.

'George, I wondered whether you would be interested in joining me in the scrap-metal business. Not just as a worker but as a partner. It would be on a strictly fifty-fifty basis. A complete split of the profits. I'm getting older and later you could take over completely.'

From a jack of all trade to a scrap-metal dealer seemed a good idea to me so I didn't hesitate, 'Yes Dad, that would be great. I promise I won't let you down. I'd love to work with you.' Some of the tension I felt in my life lifted as we sat together making plans. Sue was delighted at my new steady job. It meant security for her and the kids.

It was a new experience to walk past the large sign in Gipsy Lane. The towering office block masked the view of our working area. Day after day I went out in a van collecting scrap metal from previously arranged places. Loving my work, nobody had to ask me to make more effort. For a whole year I collected metal as Dad had always done and then began to specialise in cutting them up with an acetylene blow torch. Two machines stood in our yard. One crushed and cut up the derelict cars and sorted metals.

Dirty and sweaty, I returned home in the evenings feeling satisfied with life. I had something to aim at, I had my own business. Money was now filling my pockets. There was more to spend and so the local pub owner found me one of his regulars. Sue joined me when she could. We bought extravagant things and idolised everything we owned. It was a thrill just to spend money. When we were short of money, we would sell off our record-player or something else dirt cheap and get a bottle with it. Once we held a sale of goods, advertising in the paper. As people arrived to collect one of the items, Sue would nip out to get another bottle. By the time the last person arrived to pick up the television, we were hardly in a fit state to give it to them. Like a drug, money gripped us, or was it the drink? I didn't give it much thought.

As work prospered, I realised I needed help and soon had two men working with me. At lunch time I would pop out for a drink, and no one thought it unusual for me to be gone a while. Occasionally I went drinking with one of the men but mainly the people I worked with weren't the ones I shared my evenings with. I didn't notice much about home life; that was Sue's domain. I would cuff the kids when they were cheeky but as far as I was concerned Sue was there to keep them in order and I was there to bring in the money.

As money was my target, I was well satisfied with my life. I was making a success of everything and I didn't feel the need to be tightfisted. My home was the place I slept in. The fact that we had four kids in one bedroom didn't worry me. The colour television which arrived and the car were more important. Sue was part of the furniture, and we lived most of the time in harmony. She was still a good mate of mine and I wasn't averse to taking her on my drinking sprees. Of course sometimes she was tied up with the kids, but that didn't interfere with me. Selfish and openhearted at the same time, I lived.

3 Gipsy encounter

Sue's story...

'You'll get no repairs from me on this place. After you move, they'll get done,' the landlord threatened. The rent tribunal had been our last resort when he wanted to add £15 a week to our outgoings. We won the case but were left with a virtually derelict house on our hands. The adjoining chimney collapsed and grey tiled slates disappeared off our roof. Howling winds and driving rain wreaked further havoc. Damp seeped through the wallpaper, streaking black patterns appeared across the ceiling and down the walls. Finally, white furry mould grew under the window sills.

Our terraced house in Crombey Street had only two bedrooms. The kids were in one and we slept in the other. The white mould invaded the children's bedroom and leaking windows gradually made the room uninhabitable. We had no choice but to move all the kids into our room, which we partitioned off with an old serviceable curtain. Disturbed nights made us move downstairs into the living room. The wallpaper had a flowery pattern which was browning

with age. Our kitchen had one or two of the cup-
boards hanging precariously on the hinges. We lived
like that for a long time, but it was the straw that
broke the camel's back when the kitchen ceiling fell
in. I tackled George about it all.

'Look, George, I don't see why we have to live in
this pigsty. It's not as if we don't have the money.
You earn enough, so why don't we buy a place?'

'I'm not buying any place, woman. I'll nip down
to the Council and put my name down for one of their
houses,' George replied on his way out to the pub on
the corner.

Generous-hearted George, I thought, bitterly
knowing the scene well. As he walked through the
doors of the pub, people would crowd round him. He
was an easy touch for a drink.

'Have one on me, drinks all round,' he would
boom, waving his arms expansively. In one night
£20–£30 would go down the drain. George was
popular, everyone's idea of a mate. I could almost
here their voices, saying, 'Hi George, how's the
missus and the kids? What 'yer drinking tonight?
Pass us a fag, George – I'm out.' George always
obliged. You may meet a man in a pub, but you don't
expect him to spend most of his time in one.

My next-door neighbour babysat and sometimes I
went with him. Stories and jokes revolved around the
bar. George joined in, always trying to tell a good
one. His language was colourful and explicit. He had
a kind heart – too kind I thought, when the kids and I
wanted something. I didn't mind escaping from that
crummy house to the pub, so I could hardly blame
George for going. It was just the money flowing
through his fingers. Nagging eventually got George

to go to the Council Office.

He walked in, confident that a house would drop into his lap. For George it was just a matter of signing a form. I tried warning him before he went.

'Look, George, you know we've got the money. We've come a long way from the £12 on the building site, and then you said we were hard up. Why don't we buy one now?'

He ignored me. The woman behind the housing-office desk made reams of notes. All the usual questions about where we lived, how many kids, why he wanted to move. George read and signed the form and sat back waiting.

'Well, Mr Hayes, everything looks in order. Now I have to tell you there will be a waiting period. If you wait a minute, I'll just check for you how long!' She got up and bustled out of the room, returning about seven minutes later. George sat there puffing away at a cigarette and tapping his fingers on the desk. She bent over the desk that separated them, 'Mr Hayes, I've looked into your case and the special circumstances that meant consideration of your application. I'm afraid the waiting list is two years. We will write and notify you when there is a vacancy. It isn't necessary to come in again; it will be done automatically.'

Foul-tempered, George came home to tell me. I saw red and exploded.

'George, there is absolutely no way I'm living in this hovel for the next two years. You'll just have to get off that fat behind of yours and get out and find me a house! You'll have to buy one and spend less on your precious booze!' I swore intermittently as I gathered steam. George capitulated and began the rounds of estate agents. He finally picked on a house on a new estate. He chose it because there was only one set of neighbours to worry about. It was an end of row semi-detached with a garage. The front and back gardens had neat flower borders and plenty of lawn. The L-shaped kitchen diner gave me what I most wanted, space to breathe in a kitchen.

We moved in the worst month of the year, December. One week before Christmas, George hired a van and it took five or six trips, though we didn't have much furniture. It was tatty too.

'Take that box in the living room.' 'Put that case in our room.' 'Dump these books in Tony's bedroom.' The sergeant major issued her orders! I was in top form and felt exultant. For the first time I had my own home! It might still belong to the building society, almost lock, stock and barrel, but that was going to change. Tangibly, I had bricks and mortar that no one could throw me out of. I was left with a feeling of power as I directed all my worldly goods inside the house. '32' was home!

At teatime I fished Bryn out from between the packing cases, fed him and got him to bed. The boys appeared like a starving horde and moved in on the sandwiches and shop-bought cake.

There was a loud knock at the door. George stood there with his shirt sleeves rolled up, in his oldest jeans. He answered the front door as he was nearest. There in the porch stood a rather large lady. Her dark hair was streaked with grey. A blouse fitted over an ample bosom. Her face was set in an unwelcoming attitude.

'I just called to see you. I live next door,' she pointed to the house on our left and continued, 'I felt

I had to call round. I was told gipsies were moving in and I want to make it very clear that I won't have any bedposts, old cane or things in your garden. If you understand me, we shall get along just fine,' the gorgon firmly finished.

George was stunned but a wicked gleam entered his eye and he began to drawl in a cockney accent, 'Well, missus, I can promise you this, there'll be no scrap heap in our garden, mind you, I'm not saying the garden's not a handy place! No, that place over there is more what I had in mind.' He waved his hand towards the patch of common ground at the side of our house. 'That'll do for the broken-down cars. I can use my blow torch on them. I'll soon have them as scrap metal.' George lounged against the lintel and carried on, 'My missus will make good use of the garden, come the nice weather. You should see her outside there whittling pegs with her fag hanging out.'

Creased with laughter, I could hardly breathe! I was hidden by George's bulk so our neighbour couldn't see me. The woman, her bosom heaving slightly, mounted the attack undaunted.

'Any mess will be reported. And while I'm here, there's something else I'd like to say.'

Amused, George remarked amicably, 'Fire away, missus, anything to oblige.'

'The people who were here before you used to make a lot of noise. I had to complain about it. I hope you will refrain, this is a peaceful neighbourhood. I promise not to interfere or create a noise in return,' she concluded, folding her arms.

'My missus has a tongue in her head and she does have four kids to holler at! There's bound to be noise

but we'll try to keep it down to give you a quiet life.'
George politely and firmly finished the conversation,
'We've just moved in and are having tea, so I'm
afraid I'll have to go. I expect we'll be seeing a lot of
each other.' He shut the door and turned around to
see me bent over laughing.

'What a battle-axe,' I said, 'who does she think
she's talking to? I'm not knuckling down to her. If she
takes me on she will have met her match!'

'Come on, Gipsy Sue, let's finish tea!' George
pulled a lock of my hair.

I began to meet others who lived in the street. I
soon learned that Chloe had a reputation. She banged
on doors if there was a party and she would never
have won the best neighbour's award. No one ever
said anything to her but with me coming things were
going to change.

'Tony clear that bike out of the back garden,' I
screamed at him, 'Sebbi, where do you think you've
been?'

When Kirsty fell over and yelled as if someone was
murdering her, I was out after her and shouted,
'Crikey, what's going on here. We'll have the police
next.' Swearing, I took her inside to bathe her grazed
knee. I couldn't help noticing Chloe over the fence,
hanging out her washing. She gave me a glowering
look. Things weren't going well in that direction.

I was soon out to the dustbin dumping Georges
empty bottles next to it on the path. Chloe was
watching as usual. Nosy Parker I thought and
hollered at the kids again.

It was Sebbie who brought everything up to boiling
point. Chloe had a son, Paul, about his age. He was a

tidy, well-scrubbed boy whose face shone with too much soap. Sebbie, on the other hand, would have fitted better into a gipsy camp. I sent him out clean and he returned almost unrecognisable to me. Sebbie palled up with Paul and it looked as if their friendship might break the ice between our families, but it was not to be.

Chloe came to her door when Sebbie pulled at the letterbox.

'Can Paul come out to play?' He stood there, his shorts torn, hands grubby, a splash of mud highlighting one of his eyebrows. 'Can he come out to play over the meadow with me and my brother?' Sebbie grinned from ear to ear.

Chloe shuddered slightly and in a condescending voice she spoke,

'Just run off and play by yourself, little boy. I'm not having Paul getting into the state you're in. No, he is not coming out. Be off with you!'

Sebbie was furious as she closed the door firmly in his face. He stood there irresolute for a moment, quivering with rage and then smiled. He looked at the shiny, highly polished letterbox and the clean paintwork. Sebbie's hands were muddy and he glanced at them with satisfaction and stuck his muddy paw through the letterbox, grabbing the net curtain on the other side. He rubbed first one hand down it, then he put his other hand inside and wiped it down the curtain as well. He also kept on rattling the letterbox till our neighbour answered, running away when she appeared.

Scarlet with rage, she sounded our front door.

'That kid of yours has just run his hands over my

clean nets! He needs a good hiding! You give him one, or I will!'

'Lay a finger on my kid and you'll know it!' I screamed at her. Secretly, I was pleased as I enjoyed a good fight – it added spice to life! I was pretty sure she wasn't averse to a slanging match either. We had one on the step, and she threatened me with the police and I told her to get lost and mind her own business. My choice of words didn't reveal I was a lady.

Living with my neighbours took on a new meaning from that time. You couldn't ignore them if the kids were playing out in the front; Chloe was knocking at the door complaining. If I was yelling, she was at the rear fence smiling acidly at me and saying, 'Do you think you could make a little less noise? It used to be so peaceful round here.'

I ignored her and carried on hollering at the kids.

'You'd think she owned this place to hear her carrying on,' I would remark to George in the evening. Sometimes Chloe's husband, Steven, was sent round to us. His angular figure made a stark contrast to Chloe's plumpness. He always carried his wife's messages. My language got worse about her. George took a 'live and let live' attitude to our rows. I revelled in the details and longed to get one over on her. The kids were quite a good weapon to me. By accident, they managed to make it easy to give her a hard time. Sebbie remained friendly with Paul at school.

Chloe was a fanatic for housework. She washed her sheets three times a week and I often saw her curtains waving in the breeze. She was always out spraying the windows and rubbing them vigorously with a chamois leather. She was as obsessed about housework as my mother had been. I liked a clean house but never hoovered more than I could help. With four kids I couldn't afford to be houseproud – I would have turned myself into a nervous wreck!

George's uncle, a frail white-haired old man of seventy, came round to dig up our garden as a favour. He began digging in the front, whistling a tune. I had a grandstand view when suddenly Chloe rushed out of the house shouting loudly, 'You've got your foot in my garden! Get off, I'm calling the police! You're on my property!'

I headed towards her like a bull on the rampage.

'What do you think you're playing at? He couldn't help stepping on your garden! It was an accident.' I was hopping up and down in rage. It hadn't taken long for a couple of people to stop and stare at us. By that time the occupants in the close were getting used to our rows. Chloe stormed off into her house and although I didn't know it then, she went and rang the police.

Answering the door in the middle of the afternoon, my surprise must have shown on my face to the uniformed policeman standing there. Fred was a friend of George so I invited him into the front room.

'The inspector's had a complaint about you from your neighbour, Mrs Avon, and I've been sent round to investigate,' Fred relaxed into the armchair. After sitting down with cups of tea, I got round to explaining the circumstances of our latest row.

He approached the subject matter-of-factly, 'This is what we refer to as a domestic incident. There's very little we can do about it.' He chuckled to himself as he gazed at a picture on the wall. 'Looks to me like life is fun for you here. Stupid woman, fancy bothering us about sticking a foot in her garden! Still, I enjoyed my tea.' He got up to leave and shook my hand. 'See George and you sometime perhaps? We can have a drink together.' He left and went next door. I don't know what he said to her, but George's uncle finished the garden.

Then we were just about reaching the point where we hated the sight of each other. I would grit my teeth when I saw her and refuse to speak. George couldn't stand her either. The names he used about her were even more colourful than mine. George was in the garden one day when she heaved a bucket of water at him. George grabbed a hose and sprayed her well-dried sheets on the line. Open war was declared!

Chloe began hoovering her rooms in the evening whilst George and I were watching the television. The noise irritated us so much that we banged on the wall and went round to complain. She turned up the recordplayer, so we increased the volume of the television. Several times she called out the police. I expect they got fed up of coming, because I decided to do the same. The police couldn't do anything about it. We carried on, determined to make as much noise as possible and hit on a bright idea. We would wait until they were in bed. George and I used to sit in the evenings having a few drinks. Then we would get into bed and bang on the walls playing music and talking as loudly as possible. Sometimes we would sit and think up ways of annoying them more. My kids did that easily. Spattered with mud, they would call for Paul, and Chloe looked at them as if they were a species of animal. We argued continually about the kids. Her path was as clean as her house. The sight of one of my kids trooping up her path to the front door was enough to set off a row.

'I don't want your kids round here,' she yelled when she saw me, 'tell them to keep away from here. Can't you keep them under control?' She seemed to enjoy our rows as much as I did.

'My kids can do as they please. I don't mollycoddle them,' I said with a sneer.

I knew Chloe's greatest weakness was her pride in her house. You could pass her house and always see her doing something to it. She swept the path and tidied odd dead leaves. Everything had to be immaculate. I was wondering how to get my own back at her when an idea sprang into my mind. I reached for the telephone and dialled.

'Is that the Public Health Department? I would like to make a complaint. There's a lady at number 30, The Avenue who is being a public nuisance. It is very difficult living next to her.'

The voice at the other end of the phone spoke, 'What address was that? Yes, madam, we will see to it immediately. Just leave it to us. We will do it discreetly.' I put the phone down, laughing myself into hysteria. With growing excitement I saw the van pull up outside the house. A man in a car who looked official got out and went next door. I froze into a stationary position expecting her to turn up on my doorstep and stab me with a knife. The slam of her door rang in the street and the man walked quickly past my house without a glance. The next time I saw her she looked at me as if I was a snake coming out of a hole.

'I suppose you thought that was funny,' she

remarked icily.

'What,' I said innocently, 'I've not done anything.' She swore at me and walked off.

Time in this case didn't improve the situation. Our nightly serenades continued unabated. I lived my life trying my best to ignore Chloe, when I saw her peeping round the curtains as I went backwards and forwards with my shopping and taking the kids to and from school.

Every Wednesday I took the two younger ones to my brother's house. Paul picked me up in his car and brought me home. It was a habit over the months for him just to pull up. I would watch for him and so before he got out of the car I was there and climbing in.

Over the garden fence Chloe and I had one of our slanging matches.

'Look here, Sue, I know something that will wreck your marriage, if you don't do as I say, I'll tell George,' she said triumphantly with her feet astride and her arms folded.

'Go ahead and tell him I couldn't care less, 'I said.

George met her on his way up the garden path.

'George, could I have a word with you about Sue?' she moved eagerly towards him. With a sigh he stopped, thinking he was about to face a tirade of complaint.

'Yes, if you must,' he said tiredly.

'Sue is meeting a man every Wednesday. She gets into a car that pulls up. It's always the same man. I think she's going with him.' Chloe looked expectantly at George, watching his reaction.

'Since when has there been a law against someone

meeting their brother?' George said sarcastically, brushing past her impatiently.

'What a poisonous woman,' he said to me when he got inside the house, 'She thought your brother was your lover!' George laughed. That was one time it definitely misfired for Chloe.

Soon after that, it got to the stage where she would shout at me, 'Either you go or we leave.'

'I'm not leaving! You can go if you like, and good riddance!'

Saturday lunch time, George and I celebrated at the local pub. Both of us got tipsy and came home joking and laughing together. We giggled as we entered the house. George pulled out a piece of wood.

'Just watch me.' He took a can of paint and wrote on the board, "This house is not for sale and is not going to be." He stood back and admired his handiwork, taking a thin strip of wood he nailed it to the back of the board. Then he went out the front and at a slight angle he banged the notice into the ground. A man with a dog stopped to read and throughout the afternoon people passed, stopped and stared at it. Occasionally, we heard a laugh as one of the neighbours passed. Chloe had noticed people looking at the notice but from her house she couldn't see what was on it. Her curiosity got the better of her and she sent Paul over to have a look. She felt humiliated by what she read, but we refused to take the notice down for a week and enjoyed the chuckles of the passers-by.

Three years came and went. The feud was part of the pattern of our life. She played classical music which sounded like a dirge. I went round saying, 'Turn that off or it will be your own funeral you're going to.'

She ignored me.

I got a job as a part-time barmaid in the local pub as a break from the house, kids, husband and neighbours. George, however, still managed to haunt the pub, spending as much money as I earned working in one evening. My sense of humour made me popular there. I could always give an account of life with the neighbours to ensure everyone's attention.

George became friendly with a tall, fair-haired man called Stan. Irritated, I opened the door to find him standing there, 'Back again,' I remarked sarcastically, 'You practically live here or in the pub! George is ready as usual.' Pouring with rain or brilliant sunshine, he appeared day after day.

'You have no time for me and the kids are practically orphans,' I pleaded with George. It did no good. He just strode out of the house, linking arms with his mate. He returned in an appalling state, shirt torn and reeling in with a grin like a Cheshire cat on his face.

Seething with rage, I did nothing about it. One of the pub regulars called Jean, a peroxide blonde gave me a penetrating look and said, 'That husband of yours is eyeing up my sister and it's got to stop.'

I knew her sister's name was Sue so I didn't bother asking what she looked like. 'Stop! I'll kill him,' my language was unrepeatable. She grinned and left. I went upstairs and pulled out a dress. After hunting around for a comb, I found it, and pulled it viciously through my curls. I flung a coat over my shoulders and stormed out of the house and up to the pub in record time. George and Stan were sitting there and one look at him told me he was near the oblivion stage. He hiccoughed drunkenly when he saw me. His eyes were bloodshot as well as pale blue.

'Sue, Sue my love, how lovely to see your beautiful face.' He beamed at me and then went to turn towards the bar and lifted his arm to order a drink.

I flew at him screaming, 'Are you sure you know which Sue it is?' and clawed him with my long painted nails. The blood started to flow down his arms. Cursing, he left the pub with me and took me home. Indoors he knocked me across the room and I hit my head on the sideboard. Blood poured from my forehead, the gash was an inch long. I was almost blinded by the blood trickling down, but launching at him I clawed him again. With an oath he threw me off him. The blood was pouring down.

'I better call the hospital, Sue,' he said shamefaced, 'they'll send an ambulance.'

The ambulance came in less than six minutes and I climbed in. My dress was ripped and blood stained the collar. The driver radioed in.

'There's been a domestic incident. I'm bringing the wife in but in my opinion the husband's in a worse state.' He finished laughing heartily. I sat back satisfied.

Back home, George was suffering from his usual hangover and could hardly remember what had happened, but he had the reminders in the claw marks on his arms. Cautiously, life returned to normal and we managed to have some marital harmony. George, his usual good-natured self, made peace after his wicked act. He still bears the marks of our encounter to this day.

4   *Fear is the key*

Sue's story continues...

'Tony, Sebbie, get out of this house and off to school.'
I pulled the baby-buggy out of the cupboard.

The boys whistled past me and Tony called out,
'See you tonight, Mum.' The dishes were piled up on
the sink so I left the pushchair by the front door and
soon cleared the breakfast debris off the table. Kirsty
was playing with her doll and Bryn was still in the
high chair when I had finished. By the time I had
wiped a flannel over Bryn's face, strapped him into
the baby-buggy and buttoned Kirsty's coat, I knew I
was late.

Fed up, I left the house on that sunny morning but
the climb up the hill didn't seem too bad. I got to the
nursery breathless, worrying about missing the bus.
Mrs Jones met me at the door, a kindly middle-aged
woman and relieved me of both of them.

'Have a nice day, Mrs Hayes, see you at 2.30,' she
turned quickly, carrying Bryn and holding Kirsty by
the hand.

About twenty minutes later, the bus came and my
weekly shopping trip began. It was sheer bliss with-

out the kids but an unimaginable nightmare when they were around! Struggling onto the bus with two heavily laden bags it was a relief to see an empty seat and slide onto it. I sat next to the window and we passed the railway works and an avenue of large houses with immaculate front lawns. I couldn't help wondering how the kids were. I wasn't keen on the nursery. Most of the mums were working and left their children there all day. It seemed a dingy place. The paint seemed to be peeling off the door posts in patches. No, I wasn't that happy about them going there, but where could they go if they weren't there? The bus pulled up outside a majestic Anglican church. Two women got out and the bus moved off with a jerk. I settled back in the seat to look at the view. The bus reached a busy crossroads and we halted before a small red-bricked Victorian church. A large notice was posted outside, "Playschool here, Monday to Friday." The small print was obscured from my sight. We only stopped for a few seconds and then the bus turned the corner. I didn't attempt to get off at the Rodbourne Arms because of the groceries.

Once home, I unpacked in peace and boiled some soup up for my lunch. I put my feet up for an hour and then trailed up the hill to pick up Kirsty and Bryn. They hadn't missed me and had eaten at the nursery. Back home in time for the older boys coming in from school, there was no time to think before George got in from work. Tony and Sebbie dumped their bags and were off playing in the meadow. After having lived in a flat and a house where there was too much traffic continually whizzing past the front, our quiet close seemed like heaven to them. Mud clung to them when they turned up for tea. George arrived home with the black ground in his hands and on his overalls. It was another usual day in the household where mud and dirt seemed to rule everything. Bryn, with his tea plastered over his tee shirt, made sure my washing pile for the following day would resemble a mountain.

It was a relief to tuck the kids up in bed and grab a chair near George.

'I've been thinking about Kirsty and Bryn,' I began and passed him a cigarette.

'Huh, what's that you say, Sue?' George grunted and looked up from reading the paper.

'The kids, George, I was talking about them. I'm going to try and get them in the playgroup opposite the pub.' If I had been near enough I would have kicked him as he sat there like a complacent camel!

'You do what you think best, love,' George placidly surveyed me. He fell asleep shortly afterwards.

'I'm exhausted, George. It's been a long day. I've had enough of the kids and you can just wake up and have a conversation with me.'

'Sue, you're a pain in the neck!' he laughed. 'How about a drink? Fetch the whisky, love.'

We had an early night and I resolved to visit the playschool on the Friday while Bryn and Kirsty were at the nursery.

It was a dull day but the sun finally broke through the clouds as I made my way to the church. The playschool was tucked away behind the sombre church building with its archaic glass windows. The hut seemed filled with noise as I arrived.

'Who's running this?' I spoke abruptly to a mother who was just leaving.

'That lady over there,' she pointed to a dark, curly-haired lady who was watching a group of toddlers working with wooden puzzles. There was a pleasant atmosphere in the hut and the children were all playing happily. Helpers and mothers stood talking together. The mums seemed in no hurry to leave. It seemed different to the nursery where mothers weren't encouraged to stay. I knew without speaking to anyone that I had found the place where my two would be content and I would be happy to leave them.

The dark, curly-haired lady came towards me and shook my hand.

'My name is Mrs Hayes and I'm really looking for a playschool place for Kirsty and Bryn. Have you any vacancies?' We sat down and she spoke kindly.

'I am very sorry, Mrs Hayes. We don't have any vacancies at the moment and there is a waiting list for you to put your name on. How old are your two?'

'Kirsty's nearly four and Bryn's coming up two,' the words came out, anxiously and hurriedly.

'Your little girl is definitely old enough but I am afraid Bryn will be too young. He will have to wait a year. As soon as we have a place we will let you know. I'll take your particulars. My name is Chris.'

Efficiently she pulled a book over and began writing as I gave her our names and the children's ages. I told her my address.

'That's near where I live. You're about two streets away from me,' Chris commented as she closed the book.

'Let me know as soon as possible,' I said abruptly, standing up. I didn't like long conversations with strangers. I kept myself to myself as much as possible.

'Thanks very much, hope to hear from you soon.' She gave me a warm friendly look as I left. It had been a disappointing morning and going back to the ironing didn't help my temper! I got through the day with all of them feeling the lash of my tongue. George went off to the pub to escape so that didn't help my frame of mind.

The weekend passed uneventfully and I had just finished pegging out the washing on the Monday when the doorbell rang. Answering it quickly I knocked over a stool and moved it up against the sink before opening the door. Chris stood on the doorstep.

'Come in, Chris,' I said, surprised to see her, and ushering her into the room where plastic bricks and toys were scattered in disarray. Bryn continued playing and Kirsty ignored the visitor.

'I have come to offer you a place for Kirsty, a little boy has had to leave. Would you like it?' Chris sat down in the armchair.

'You said you had a waiting list. Why are you offering it to me then?' Suspicious, but rather pleased, I asked the question.

'You seemed rather desperate and we really thought your need was greater with two toddlers,' Chris smiled with genuine warmth. Relaxed, I offered her a cup of tea and she left shortly afterwards.

Kirsty's going to playschool changed my routine, but I didn't care because I had what I wanted. The playschool staff always appeared very friendly though I was practically a stranger to them. I gained the impression they wanted to talk to me but I wasn't inclined to be pally and day after day I left Kirsty and returned to pick her up scarcely speaking to anyone. Abrupt and to the point I commented, giving my opinion when it was asked of me!

Bryn going to playschool as well marked a change in my attitude. I became a little curious about the ladies, who I discovered had children in the group. They were all mums running the morning sessions and they went along to the Baptist church but they didn't talk about religion to me. The children began singing 'running over, running over, my cup's full and running over.' As a change from nursery rhymes it didn't seem too bad. It also seemed more of a preparation for school. Kirsty was about to start infant school and because she enjoyed playschool so much there didn't seem to be any problem for her future. Bryn never kicked up a fuss about going and things were running smoothly when I began feeling unwell.

Since Bryn had been born I had off and on experienced a sharp stabbing pain in my groin. It came on when my monthly cycle was due. I just accepted it, otherwise I had a healthy dislike of being sick and had little time with four kids to think of doing anything about it.

I started waking in the morning and rushed to the bathroom. The diarrhoea quickly passed and the rest of the day was free of trouble. I felt really ill and everything was becoming too much effort. My stomach began to swell and embarrassing though it was, I looked about five months pregnant. Early each morning I passed diarrhoea and as the days passed fear entered my life.

'Look, Sue, go to the doctor,' George said emphatically.

I shrank from going and replied, 'I just can't. What if it's something serious?'

'It's better to get it over with and find out so you can get fixed up,' George, practical as usual, insisted.

The doctor gave me a brief examination feeling my stomach and prodding it slowly. I sat tensely in the chair.

'It looks like a simple case of food poisoning, Mrs Hayes. I'll just write you up some tablets. We'll soon have you as right as rain,' he said comfortingly.

Happily I got out of the surgery feeling as if a weight had been lifted from my mind. I told George what he said.

'See, I told you not to worry, Sue,' he replied confidently, 'Just take it easy.'

Faithfully I took the tablets, but my stomach remained swollen and the diarrhoea continued. I had little choice but to go back a second time. Dismayed, I waited for his verdict.

'Mrs Hayes, it looks to me as if you are suffering from a severe case of indigestion. Eat your meals slowly and take your medicine before meals and it will right itself.' The doctor spoke confidently and reassuringly and my secret panic began to evaporate. Nothing to worry about, I thought. I took the prescription to the chemist who measured out a chalk-white liquid into a bottle. Relieved, I went back to the children, the housework and my husband. But not for long, I was back again.

The doctor patiently spoke into my fears, 'Mrs Hayes, you have a straightforward case of indigestion. Just try to remain calm and don't worry. It will eventually clear up of its own accord!'

With heartfelt relief I left the surgery clutching the prescription. The chemist measured me out some more chalk-like liquid into a bottle. George chatted on about some woman at work who had had similar problems. I pushed the nagging doubts to the back of my mind and carried on. Shopping, ironing, taking Kirsty and Bryn to playschool, seeing Tony and Sebbie off to school, I couldn't shake off the conviction that I was ill. The diarrhoea stopped but I began bleeding irregularly, and my stomach was still swelling. I went back to the doctor, as there didn't seem anything else to do.

'Mrs Hayes, your trouble is still indigestion. The irregularity of your cycle is only to be expected in a woman of your age. You've had four children, haven't you? The more you worry the worse it will get. Take life easy and you will soon get back to normal.'

In the wake of such confidence I wasn't able to express my own doubts. George quoted some woman at work. It was all so depressing. I didn't want to think about it. The bleeding continued and lethargy set in. Everything was an effort of will to do. I felt ill, but apart from being pale, I didn't look too bad on the outside. Yet what I felt inside was a different matter. I didn't get better naturally, so I went back to the doctors. His face when he saw me gave me the distinct impression that I wasn't very welcome! He gave me the usual quick examination and reached a rapid diagnosis.

'Mrs Hayes, given time I am sure your problem will clear up. It will take its course.' He ended by giving me a prescription for the medicine. It was a wonder I wasn't addicted by that point. He added a tonic to buck me up a bit. A few weeks later I was back still suffering from a swollen stomach and bleeding without warning. I didn't have any faith in a cure any more but I carried on going to the doctor because I didn't know what else to do. The diarrhoea came and went along with the bleeding. I felt I was in a mess and secretly worried as it continued.

At thirty I was the mother of four kids. Still young, I didn't want to have to be ill any longer than I could help. From the October to the Christmas I was bleeding and feeling miserable.

George had got a couple of tickets for a dinner and dance at work. The thought of going made me shudder. It was my idea of tortue to talk to snobby women and listen to long speeches with only one thing in common – they were all so boring! Bad food and posh folk would ruin my evening.

George wouldn't take no for an answer, so I couldn't get out of going. He even handed me the cash to get a new long dress. Miserably, I trailed round various shops, dresses stuck to my figure. After trying on more dresses than I could count without success, I realised I had to try the maternity department.

A long maternity dress carefully concealed my swelling figure and I purchased it hoping no one would ask when the baby was due. Christmas was busy as usual and I didn't have much time to think about the dance until it was nearly upon us.

I woke the morning we were going to the ball with a thumping head. George had left for work before I discovered I was haemorrhaging. My bleeding was so bad I crawled onto the sofa and spent the day indoors. I got up as little as possible and watched the kids. I was thinking I just couldn't go on llike this, but I knew George would never believe me. He would just think I was putting it on. Anyway, he enjoyed the booze-up that always followed at 2.30 am when the drinks were free. Enduring the three-hour speeches and slow dances brought its own reward for George. Normally, I too, only went for the drink, but he had a funny sense of duty towards women and wouldn't dream of missing the dance anyway. George was more sociable than me.

Bleeding heavily and without telling George, I prepared for the dinner dance. He was busy with his cuff links and tie, so he didn't notice the fact I was subdued as we got ready. Splashing perfume on, I descended the stairs slowly, when giddiness temporarily made me stop.

'Come on, we'll be late if you don't get a move on! It's starting at 6.30,' George said impatiently. I couldn't rush, so George became more and more irritated. Relief flooded me as I climbed into the passenger seat of the car. The giddiness passed off, George talked and I listened.

'Nearly everyone will be there. All the usual crowd, you know most of their wives,' he said. 'And I don't like them much,' I was thinking.

Pulling into the car park we came to rest next to a Daimler. It was that sort of evening. The room was crowded with women in long dresses. Long dangling earrings and expensive necklaces hung on them. Men in dinner jackets stood around. Occasionally one was puffing at a cigar. 'Let me out of here,' I thought, but didn't say anything. George with a rather plastic smile was greeting people, he knew them all! It was as if I was looking at a reflection in a pool, it just wasn't real to me.

The dinner card was printed with our names and showed us clearly where we were to sit. A few slightly wilted flowers were in a vase in the centre of the table. George ignored me, talking to the man on his right. I was glad he did because I felt awful and really weak. The dinner was terrible, coarse undercooked cabbage and tough meat. I picked at it, my mouth felt dry and I was feeling thirsty. The speeches were given in low monotonous tones. The giddiness swept across me in waves and I began to feel quite cold and shivery, though the bodies around me increased the temperature of the room. I just couldn't help shivering occasionally.

We got up from the table to dance but I felt I just couldn't.

A woman in a long red dress whom I knew slightly looked at me with concern, 'Would you like to go to the cloakroom?' You're looking very pale.'

'Yes, please,' I mumbled taking her arms, swaying slightly. At the washroom I half-collapsed. Seated for a while didn't make me feel any better.

'You shouldn't have come. You're obviously ill,' she said, 'I'll get your husband, you need to get home to bed.'

George hadn't been aware that I was sick. Before I had come, I doubted whether he would have believed me. He knew I hated these functions.

George took one look at my pale, drawn face and said, 'Let's go home, girl, you can see the doctor on Monday.'

He bundled me into the car and we made record time home. I spent the rest of the weekend in bed, feeling washed out and uncomfortable. It passed through my mind that perhaps I could go up to the hospital but I dismissed it. No, I would wait until Monday. The appointment on Monday morning was with my own doctor.

'I still don't think there is much wrong with you. If you took the pills your periods might be more regulated.'

I went home to George who dismissed what he said, 'Look, Sue, it's obvious you aren't right. We'll have to try another doctor. Make another appointment.'

I saw a nice younger doctor who asked me immediately if I was sure I wasn't pregnant. Boldly I said, 'No.'

'Now think carefully, Mrs Hayes. Is there any chance you could be?'

I explained to him carefully about the bleeding and told him it was an impossibility. He accepted everything I said and didn't imply I was imagining my symptoms.

'I will have to give you an examination. If you will just get up onto the couch it won't take long,' the doctor assured me when he noticed my reluctance. He moved his hands first of all gently around my stomach area and then he did an internal. 'I can feel something. It's about five and a half inches in diameter. You may have fibroids or an ovarian cyst. I am going to have to send you to the hospital.'

Fear gripped me at the word "hospital". What about the kids?

'Does that mean I need an operation?' I enquired hesitantly.

'Most likely, but you need not worry. I can assure you, afterwards you will definitely be back to normal,' he smiled.

Within a few days I was up at the hospital visiting specialists. I underwent a scan and blood tests. The specialist confirmed my fears.

'I am sorry, Mrs Hayes, you are going to have to come in and have an operation. It is a case for surgery. You will be in about fourteen days. We will let you know as soon as a bed is available.'

Panic imprinted itself on me. What about Kirsty and Bryn? How would George and I cope? George had the work to run, he couldn't just take time off because I was ill. Fear made me feel a bit sick. The thought of being cut up was a shock, and I went home in a daze. George told me about a woman at work with fibroids.

'Apparently it's quite common, love. You don't have to worry yourself. The doctors will sort you out. Have you thought of asking your friend Lynn to have the kids?'

Rushing around making arrangements in between keeping going with everyday life made the time pass quickly.

Chris dressed in her usual slacks met me at the doorway of the hut. She seemed to me a comforting familiar presence. She must have noticed how worried and the strain I was under, because she drew me on one side and remarked, 'Do you feel like sharing what's the matter?' She spoke gently and quietly. Her dark eyes showed such a genuine concern that it was with relief I just began to talk and talk. It all poured out of me in a flood.

'I've found out I've got to go into hospital, there's talk of me having a hysterectomy. The doctor seems to think I'll be there for a few days. George is tied up at work and can't get the time off. I don't know what I can do.' I stopped for breath before continuing. Christine didn't interrupt, 'You see it's Kirsty and

Bryn, I don't know what's going to happen to them. They seem too small to leave.'

Finishing lamely and close to tears, I felt and looked uptight. Exhausted with emotion, it was a good release to share my fears.

'Maybe I could help you there. I don't mind looking after Kirsty and Bryn, they're sweet kids. They're also used to me. Look, I don't think you need to worry – just get your husband to drop them off with me. If I can't do it, then one of the other ladies will help me out. At least the children know us,' Chris smiled confidently at me.

'Well, that's very kind of you. I mean I hardly know you at all.' I couldn't think of words to express my thanks. I was really surprised at her offer. Somehow I never expected kindness from anyone. I had been often struck by the trouble the helpers took with the children. It hadn't taken me very long to realise that they really meant the small gestures of concern they showed to mothers and children. It was when they actually showed the same concern for me that I was rather surprised and a bit embarrassed. I left feeling rather bewildered but a bit better.

I met a lady called Delia from the playgroup. She was one of the helpers and she had heard I was going into hospital. She stopped and spoke to me outside the playschool.

'The Lord has laid your name on my heart to pray for you. I want you to know I and the others will be praying for you.'

I must have stared at her, it must have been about the most unusual thing ever said to me. None of them had ever said anything remotely Christian sounding to me before. I didn't quite know how to reply and grunted my thanks. Inwardly I was in turmoil, wondering what she meant. Could God possibly be interested in me? It seemed hardly likely. Still it was a kind thought. The words drummed in my mind as I prepared to go into hospital. They came back to me unbidden, "The Lord has laid your name on my heart." What on earth had she meant? Fancy anyone praying for me – tough, hard Sue, who made my own way in the world! I had taken a few hard knocks in my time but had always got around to giving as good as I got.

There is nothing that brings you more rapidly down to size than a hospital bed. Stripped and dressed in a new cotton nightie I wondered what to do. A nurse made me get into bed while I waited for the doctor. I was quaking with fear. George turning up with flowers made me feel even more of an invalid. I was on a one-way ticket to the operating table and it was too late to pull back.

5　*Out of the darkness*

Sue's story continues...

They dosed me up with Valium to calm my fears and I lay in bed at the far end of the ward gazing out of the window. Someone trundled past pushing a laundry trolley. I saw patients going to X-ray. Inside the icy grip of fear gnawed at my stomach. The only other times I had been in hospital were to have my babies. Tony was now eleven and Bryn three and a half. Waves of panic kept on washing over me.

Chris walked up the ward towards me wearing a dress with a silver cross and chain around her neck and Delia walked behind her, smiling gently. They gave me cards and sat down after pulling up two chairs to the side of the bed.

'You're looking a bit worried. Can we help you?' Delia said leaning forward to rest her elbows on the thin cotton blankets.

'Just say what you like,' Chris said, 'We'd like to help. It seems a nice ward.' There were some flowers on the window sill near my bed which a visitor had left.

The fears within me surfaced and I began to talk,

63

stumbling over my words and close to tears. But I had a sympathetic audience.

'I have been lying here thinking and worrying. What about George and the kids? What if he goes on one of his drinking binges and just leaves the kids in the house on their own? Chris, you know what he's like, he's never had to cope on his own with the kids. I've always been there. Oh God, what if he neglects them and I'm just lying here doing nothing?'

My face was chalk-white and the signs of illness were also clearly visible. My eyes were screwed up and my cheeks hollowed out. I pushed my hair nervously from my face.

Chris answered gently, 'Sue, look this is what friends are for, to help out. Leave us to sort out about the kids for you. I heard you were paying someone to look after the kids and do your washing and ironing. Tell George to give it all to me. I'll do it. The only important thing is that you get well.'

I breathed a sigh of relief,

'I don't know why you are doing it but I want to thank you. I'm really grateful.'

When Delia got up I couldn't help thinking of the words she had said to me before I had come into hospital. 'The Lord has laid your name on my heart.' She was such a nice lady but what a stupid thing to say! As if God was interested in me! I wasn't too sure He was around either.

Chris stopped as they were leaving, 'The other ladies of the playgroup and myself will be praying for you. I'll come and see you after your operation when you're getting better.'

When they had left, my fears returned. I couldn't stop them tormenting me. More Valium was given to calm me as I waited for the operation to remove the ovarian cyst and the fibroids.

Fatalistically I was wheeled down to the operating table after having my pre-med. Fear hadn't kept the operation day away.

I woke and drifted in that half-land of waking and sleeping. Like a drowning man, my life flashed before me, and then I passed into the emptiness of sleep.

As I woke again, my pain had intensified and I wondered, 'Why didn't they let me die? I'm in so much pain.' Regularly the nurses came and gave me injections to take away the pain. My mind was muddled after having them. Faces meant nothing to me, they just blurred before me. I wanted to be left alone. George must have sat by my bed but I didn't take any notice of him. For a short while I lived in my own world in semi-darkness. Pain was the only companion to the periodic euphoria that set in as the injections punctured my skin. I emerged from my nightmare slowly and from sips of water gradually graduated to soup and from soup to small quantities of food. It took a few days. I still felt very ill. Doctors came at intervals to examine me. Now I noticed my painful thinness. My bump was gone. The only bit of me I was able to admire was my legs. There was no fatness anywhere to be seen. I waited to get better.

George was often there from the pub and he sat gazing into my eyes and clasping my hand tightly. Love blazed from his eyes along with a measured look of pain. I was comforted.

'How are the kids, George?' I said conversationally.

George remarked absentmindedly, 'The kids, oh they're all well. I'm getting quite a bit of help. Sue, it will be good to have you home.'

I saw the tears start in his eyes but he turned away from looking at me and focused his attention on the wall. I didn't comment because I was feeling very tired and wanted to sleep. Instead I closed my eyes wearily and George soon tiptoed away. After speaking to the sister he left.

The ten days after my operation passed slowly. It was a time of surprises, my brother came sometimes with George and sometimes alone. He would sit there for two or three hours by my bed. His hand was covering mine. His devotion was unexpected and worrying. I was never short of visitors. It started when first one schoolfriend came and then another. I hadn't seen some of them for years. One good friend of mine even turned up with her mother. We talked lightly.

'How's your work going? I heard you got married but it didn't work out.'

She replied, 'I'm fine. No, my marriage was a flop but I picked up the pieces and am carrying on. I hope you get out of here soon.'

As she left I reflected on events. I was in a ward filled with beds. You knew you were getting better after an operation because your bed was gradually moved nearer and nearer the door. Worry consumed me as they didn't shift my bed. The constant stream of visitors made me feel insecure. Why did all these people I hadn't seen for years keep on visiting me? My brother sitting there didn't seem right either. George came in more often drunk than sober and sat with a rather fixed smile on his face. They were all keeping something from me but I didn't want to think what. I didn't ask questions because I was afraid of the answer. I tried cracking jokes with the visitors and spoke superficially to everyone. The plastic front hid the turmoil of emotions.

I wasn't worried about the kids because George reported regularly how well things were running at home. That was at least one worry I could shelve.

The specialist came to see me on the tenth day and I remember vaguely George sat by the bed as he spoke seriously to me.

'Mrs Hayes, I'm afraid that I've bad news for you.' I sat up in bed and listened attentively to what he had to say although I didn't want to hear it. 'When we operated on you we found you didn't have an ovarian cyst, we removed a large growth. It was so big that we weighed it. It was eight and a half pounds. Further tests revealed that it was cancerous. We can do treatment for you. It involves radium. It is like having X-rays. The treatment will last a few weeks.'

The specialist said it all kindly but impersonally. A torrent of helplessness flooded into me and engulfed me. Then I realised just what the stream of visitors had been for and the significance of my unmoved bed and my brother's constant presence. I was going to die! I was never leaving the hospital. Everybody knew the hospital was going to be my tomb and the next stop would be the mortuary.

I didn't notice the specialist leave. For the second time my world was falling apart. George's well-loved face was before me. We had always loved, fought and loved again. Pictures flooded into my mind of my children. I ached as I thought of how young they all were and what we had shared together. The times when we had been hard up and finding enough food had been a problem. Now money wasn't a problem, I had to go and leave them. My thoughts were lonely, bitter and desolate. My experience was so personal that even George couldn't penetrate it and bring comfort. I tried hard to cling to George in the darkness. George hit the bottle for support!

It was on a cold and blustery day that Chris and Carol (another lady from the playgroup) came to visit me. They already knew I had cancer and their hearts went out towards me as they saw my obvious distress. Naturally and without awkwardness they began to talk about their faith. I listened out of the desperation of a dying woman. I was seeking a way of escape.

Christine spoke first of how she had found God to be her friend. He had cared for her when she had lost her way and even ran away from Him. He never deserted her. She finished by saying, 'You know, Sue, Jesus can heal you.'

Carol carried on as soon as she stopped. 'I, too, know that the Lord is alive and giving my life to Him was just the beginning. After being a Christian for sixteen years, I had a new experience of God which revolutionised my life. Later I was healed. I had been deaf in my left ear and God took away my deafness.'

'Your God seems to work,' I said wondering. 'I think I would like to know him.'

Chris and Carol were still talking to me and had explained that their new pastor was coming to see me. As they were talking about it, he came along the ward. He was of medium height and had a pleasant kindly face. He just didn't fit in with my idea of a minister and a little confused and embarrassed I sat up higher in the bed, tugging at my nightdress to make sure it was in order. He came over and I was struck by the gentleness in his voice as he spoke to me. I had met his Canadian wife, Sylvia, before through the playgroup, but for us it was our first meeting.

The pastor moved to the left-hand side of the bed and pulled up a chair sitting close to the locker with the get-well cards and my water jug on it. Chris and Carol explained to him of my interest in Christianity.

He told me that Jesus was on the outside of my heart knocking, his eyes smiled and I felt the gentleness flowing out of him as he talked.

'Sue, do you really want to accept Jesus Christ as your personal Saviour and Lord? Think carefully before you answer.' I wasn't hesitating, my life was ruined. I was a condemned woman. I had to know God and to find him.

'Yes, I want to be a Christian,' I said abruptly and confidently. I just didn't care that I was in an open ward where everybody could see me. I needed a Jesus who was alive!

'Please pray after me this prayer,' Reg, the pastor, continued.

Propped up on my starched pillows and oblivious of everyone but the pastor, I shut my eyes and concentrated.

'Dear Lord Jesus, I know I am a sinner, I have done many things wrong. I want to give my life to you. Please come into my life and change me.'

'Now thank God for doing that — thank Him for coming into your life,' Reg said quietly and gently. He was smiling at me. My prayer tumbled out, I was just beginning my relationship with God.

When I had finished my prayer, my eyes flew open

and I shifted up the bed. After straightening up, I said in my usual, abrupt no-nonsense manner, 'Well, what about this healing?' Carol was a little shocked, Christine was thinking perhaps God could do it, and the pastor was confident. At that moment George strode up the ward with a swagger. His bloodshot eyes and slightly blurred voice told me he had been drinking. Christine noticed also. George and Reg had met in the corridors of the hospital briefly. George came up to me and stood by my head. Reg and Carol stood side by side on the left of me and George joined Christine on the right. Christine moved down the bed a bit to let George near me.

'George, I've got something to tell you, I've just become a Christian. I want to go to church.' I looked happily towards him.

George smiled tolerantly at me, 'That's just fine Sue. I only want you to be happy; you can go to church if you like.' New hope for my life probably filled him with relief as I had been so morbid before.

'George, your wife would like us to pray for her healing. Have I your permission to pray with her? I will pray for her and anoint her with this oil.' He pulled out a small bottle from his pocket.

George said dully, 'I don't see it can do any harm.'

To take away any embarrassment and awkwardness the curtains surrounding my bed were pulled around. George, Reg, Christine and Carol and I were hidden from the curious eyes of the other patients in the gynaecological ward. I sat there not knowing what to expect. Geroge held my hand tightly, and a slight smell of drink hung in the air.

Carol and Christine moved closer towards me and

Reg came and placed his hand on my head. Both Carol and Christine also joined him in placing their hands on me.

It was then that I felt as if my head was opening up and this hot liquid was being poured into me. Soon it felt as if it was oozing out of my pores. Reg had placed the oil on my forehead and Carol and Christine were praying in a language I didn't know. The hot liquid was filling every space in my body, but suddenly I began to panic as I felt it gushing out between my legs. I shifted uncomfortably in the bed and lifted the covers and pushed my hand down onto the patch of bed. Embarrassed, I whispered to Carol, 'I think I've wet the bed.' I carried on cautiously feeling with my hand. The bed was dry. 'No, I haven't, there's nothing there.'

From that moment I knew with inner certainty that I had been healed. I rested in contentment. The heat passing through me was bringing healing to me. George felt nothing but the glow of health, exuberant joy and wholeness that had taken hold of me.

'Don't worry, George, I shall be allright. Jesus has healed me.' George didn't stop looking worried nor did he believe me.

The pastor, Carol and Christine were watching my radiant face. They were all thrilled at my confidence in God and the certainty I had that I had been healed.

My curtains were pulled back and I was once again in the open ward, breathing the air of liberation from the fear of death. Death had lost its grip on me, and I was free to live again.

My life had been changed. My temperature had been high and an unknown fever had enveloped me before their visit. The doctors had been puzzled as to the source of the infection. After they left, it had gone. Within forty-eight hours, no trace of my sickness remained.

George took me home and both he and the hospital doctors wanted me to take the radium course. I didn't need it but I had to take it. After each session I knew only an abundant health. Instead of feeling unwell and needing rest, I went shopping with my sister-in-law and did all the things I wanted to do with more enjoyment, for now I was living a new life.

My enthusiasm overwhelmed everybody. I couldn't stop talking about my new-found faith to anyone who would listen! George was treating me with patience, still feeling my last hour was coming rapidly. It was so good to be home with the children. I knew I would watch them growing up. I had the precious gift of life and I could lift my voice in a laugh of pure happiness. What had nearly slipped from me had come back with more meaning than before. Cancer was still in the world but not in me. The old has passed away and the new had come! I could skip, jump and run like a child!

Faith entered my life and took away the hardness and impenetrable barrier I built to shield me from the world. The miracle of my salvation had been followed minutes later by the miracle of healing. The woman who had loved only the few had found the One who loved the world! His sacrifice on the cross was giving me day-by-day real life. It is almost too marvellous to put into words!

Many did not believe I had been healed so I could hardly blame George for his attitude. My children accepted me as I was. They never thought of the future without me. Mum had come home to stay.

My check-ups at the hospital passed uneventfully. I didn't fall sick and no trace of cancer cells was around. Yearly, these trips carried on to the hospital.

Time was to prove to people that I had truly been healed. I didn't want to go along to church without George and the kids, so I decided not to go. Instead I went along to the weekly ladies' meetings where we shared our lives and studied the Bible. I kept on learning more and more about what it meant to be a Christian. I felt pity for George who was unable to accept my healing and faith. His story is very different to mine, as we shall now see.

6 *Don't bump her off, Lord!*

George's story...

Sue had her operation on February 24th 1977, and I made the pub my home for the day. I found a small pub close to the town centre and a sympathetic barman and just sat there drinking lager after lager.

When I phoned the hospital ward from the pub the sister answered cautiously, 'Mr Hayes, we would rather not discuss your wife over the phone, we would like you to come up and see the surgeon in charge of your wife's case.'

The hesitation in her voice made warning bells ring in my mind as I practically threw the telephone down. I said to no one in particular, 'Oh God, don't let Sue die!'

When I got to the ward I was ushered into a side ward and the surgeon was sent for. To my surprise she was a lady.

'Mr Hayes, I am afraid we have some bad news for you. This morning we removed an eight-and-a-half pounds growth. Take a seat,' she said before continuing.

Bewildered and frightened, I sat down heavily on

the chair.

'The tumour was malignant. In layman's terms that means your wife has cancer. We took out all that we could but we didn't dare carry on because your wife couldn't have coped with it. At this moment in time the best we can offer you is that she may live two years. She will go on for so long and then deteriorate.'

In a strange way I felt it wasn't just Sue's death sentence that had been delivered but my own also. I shivered although I wasn't cold, and then anger mingled with my grief.

'I am going to go down to that stupid doctor and I'm going to put him in the same place as Sue,' I said. My face was suffused with rage. I was like a time bomb close to explosion.

The surgeon remained calm and spoke quietly, "Mr Hayes, whatever you do to that doctor wouldn't make your wife better. Doctors are fallible. Concentrate on helping your wife. Revenge won't do that.' She stayed with me trying to calm my rage and after a while I grew quieter, though my bitterness remained for the doctor who thought my wife had wind when she had cancer. 'Mr Hayes, would you like us to tell your wife now?' I shrugged but quickly came to a firm decision.

"I don't want her to be told yet. Let me talk this over with her brothers. I think they should be told first and then we will decide about Sue.'

'I hope you won't take long about deciding. I have always found it's better to tell the person concerned. Your wife is going to need all the support you can give her. Your wife,' she continued with emphasis, 'hasn't got long to live.' I swallowed convulsively, tightening my fingers on the chair until my knuckles whitened.

'We'll do anything you say.'

Her calm eyes scrutinised my unhappy face,

'I know this has been very difficult for you. We will do all we can for your wife. I can assure you, she is in good hands now. The next thing to be done is that she must have radium treatment. This will slow down the growth of the cancer cells and destroy them.'

I didn't want to break down in front of her and escaped as quickly as I could. It was a case of the quickest route to the nearest pub and I drank myself close to oblivion before visiting Sue. I wasn't drunk enough to forget facing her. Her death sentence haunted me. My life was ripped savagely apart. Cancer must be one of the worst words in the English language. Any tears I shed were into a pint of beer. Before Sue, I played the part of the cheerful husband expecting a fit wife to come home. Pain pierced every word I spoke and I dreaded Sue seeing through my façade.

I rang Sue's brothers and they came round to see me. Their shock equalled mine. Ideas bounced around the living room.

'Take her to Harley Street, between us we'll find the money.'

'I don't understand it but I've heard some people are cured at Lourdes. Try there.'

I'd rather trust the best doctors. Surely something can be done for Sue.'

'One thing I know, you can't have something like cancer and not know about it. Sue has got to be told. She will guess soon enough and then she'll distrust us all and feel we've betrayed her.'

It was the conversation of desperate people.

'I'll let the surgeon know. The doctors can tell her. After that it is up to us to do what we can to make her as comfortable as possible,' I finished with a sigh. I was exhausted by my emotions.

Sue was told and I sat there strained and tired by her bedside. The dreaded word "cancer" passed between us. Her agony and fear made me, a 5 ft 8 inch muscular man, feel helpless and weak. The misery was too agonising to watch. I wanted the bottle to take away the pictures from my mind. I didn't need other people as I needed Sue. She was my rough diamond and I would have exchanged any ransom for her at that moment. I was determined to give her whatever I could to make her happy.

I met the pastor Reg with Sue. When she was prayed for by the minister, I hoped it comforted her but it held little comfort for me. A woman wearing glasses at Sue's bedside spoke to me. Sue had become a Christian, then I was alone in my distress. Carol, the woman, approached me, laying a hand on my shoulders.

'George, the Lord has told me you are going to become a jewel in His crown. The Lord is really going to use you and Sue.'

I inched away from her quickly thinking, 'Stupid woman, the Lord – if He's around – wouldn't use me. I'm too wicked!' I bore it in mind to avoid the woman if I ever saw her again. No one else commented before the visitors left. Sue thought she was healed, but I knew better, for the specialist had given her a death warrant. She was expected to come out of hospital but to deteriorate rapidly after that. I couldn't doubt the expert.

Sue now believed in God. She had faith and happiness combined and she began to soften visibly before my eyes. She seemed more vulnerable and approachable. Her heart was opened to God and opened to me. She came out of a hospital a different person to the one who went in. When she left the hospital she looked about the healthiest person I had ever seen. She radiated glowing health. Already she was gaining lost weight and had a teenaged shaped figure. Her hair had begun to shine and her eyes smiled brightly into mine.

'George, I have never felt better! Isn't the Lord good to me?' she explained on our way home in the car.

'Yes, love,' I said hurriedly, 'You look OK.' I ignored her reference to her new-found faith. The specialist's words kept the barrier of unbelief in my mind. It was true she looked healthy, but appearances could be deceptive. I grieved inwardly as I thought of the future without Sue. What would I do with four growing kids on my own? The oldest was only eleven. There would be no one to share my joys and sorrows. I just wanted to drink to forget it all.

Sue was wanting to mix with other Christians. I felt threatened by her going to church and so she didn't go, but I could hardly object to her going along to a weekly ladies' meeting held in the afternoon. I did want her to live out her last months with peace of mind.

'O.K., Sue, go along. I don't see what you find so interesting about these Christian get-togethers, but I don't want to stop you if it makes you happy,' I said complacently. I didn't let it interfere with my life.

My toleration extended to Sue leaving Christian

books around the house. Occasionally when I found one on the coffee table or on the sofa I would pick it up and have a read. Of course I always checked Sue wasn't around to see me doing it. I never remembered afterwards what I had read.

While Sue had been in hospital I had seen our neighbour Chloe and her husband Steven. They were in the back garden. Chloe was quite shaken when she heard the word 'cancer'. She didn't wish that fate on her enemy.

'I am sorry to hear that. I hope she comes home soon,' she said before going back inside her house.

When Sue came home, her own hatred for her neighbour had disappeared. She felt love take its place, and now she cared for her neighbour. As soon as she saw Chloe outside, she went towards her deliberately.

'Thanks for asking after me. How are you?'

'I'm fine. I hope you're feeling better after the op. You are feeling better aren't you?' she enquired carefully.

'Oh yes, my life has been changed. I've become a Christian and I know that God has healed me completely.' Sue's confident tone must have embarrassed her neighbour who made some excuse to go back into her house.

Chloe had listened unbelievingly to Sue, and had just politely wished her well as she went inside her house.

Sue didn't change her mind about Christianity and she began to read her Bible and pray to God as if He were her friend. Puzzled, I remained unconvinced, going off alone on my drinking sprees. It was a year of money, drink and a more peaceful home life fore me.

One Saturday evening I returned from the pub bringing a bottle of booze home. Sue was waiting for me as usual and we sat in the living room. She was watching the television. I felt quite suddenly this overwhelming desire to go to church. I really wanted to go and so I said to a half distracted Sue,

'I've got to go to church and I'm going tomorrow.'

Sue grinned across at me, 'Why don't we go along to the Baptist church then tomorrow?'

'No, I'm not going there. I'm going to find my own. I just feel I've got to get to a church. I think I'll go now, and then I'll know the times of the services.'

Sue didn't comment as I left. I drove the car up to Rodbourne and around the roundabout where I saw an impressive church building. I drew up at the kerb, got out, there was no notice giving the times of services. I wandered up the path through the grave-stones. There was no notice there giving the times of the services. St Mary's Anglican church looked interesting. I wandered around the outside but no sign indicated the information I wanted. 'That's it, I am not going to church,' I thought as I got into my car. I went up the road to the crossroads and my car stopped outside the Baptist church. A notice seemed to stand out, 'Morning service 11 a.m.'

I got back to Sue, 'Well love, it looks like you've won! I'm going to the Baptist church tomorrow.' I was feeling quite cheerful after making my decision.

'George, let's all go together, you, me and the kids,' Sue said eagerly.

'No, definitely not. I'm going on my own,' I said firmly and, a bit more kindly, I explained my reasons. 'Look, Sue, I'm going alone to find out what kind of people they are. If all six of us troop in there and I don't like it, then we're stuck. I can't get out quick enough.'

Sue was disappointed but she had to accept it. I woke early on the Sunday morning sober and still wanting to go.

I got to the church and placed myself strategically close to the door for a quick getaway. I knew it would be easier there to leave and if I stayed until the end of the service I didn't want to be waylaid by any of Sue's enthusiastic friends. For me, church was the place where sinners went every Sunday with their long faces to do penance for their sins. They needed to go. The service began and I looked around the congregation. The people looking happy impressed me. Some seemed tipsy. I settled more comfortably back into the pew. They sang choruses, some raised their hands in the air. No, I had nothing to bother about here. They were a nice bunch if a bit fanatical. Sue and I and the kids could come along together. Church wasn't that bad after all! I flung a few coins in the collection and escaped after the last hymn was sung.

I went into the pub opposite the church straight after the service. A mate of mine, with whom I had been drinking for years, was at the bar before me. I approached him and he ordered a lager for me.

'Where have you been George?' he said, stroking the stubble on his chin.

'I've just been to church. It wasn't what I was expecting. The people were a cheerful bunch. It didn't resemble a funeral parlour at all. For a bunch of sinners they seemed remarkably cheerful about it,'

I said swigging the rest of the lager down. It was my turn so I bought the next round.

'Me, I never go to church. Oh, I've been to a wedding and even a funeral,' Bill remarked thoughtfully, 'I don't want to go though.'

'I had this sudden urge to see what church was like for myself,' I said, feeling the drink beginning to take effect.

'Are you going again?' he said when we were beginning our fourth pint together.

'I think I might,' I said after hesitating slightly. Bill started talking about his week at work and nothing else was said. Happily drunk, I went back to Sue. The dinner was dried up and, needless to say, she wasn't pleased with me.

'Next week we'll all go to church. I quite enjoyed myself at the Baptist church,' I said to pacify her.

'I hope you don't change your mind,' she said, thumping the plate on the table.

The following Sunday we all sat near the door of the church. I looked around at the tipsy looking congregation. I thought of them all as smiling hypocrites, probably two-faced, who smartened themselves up to come to church.

They were sitting with their clean polished faces. I had few thoughts about God. I thought death was the end of life. If there was such a thing as heaven I wasn't getting there and had severe doubts that any of the smiling bunch around me was going either. Sue greeted everyone after the service, but I quickly got out of the door. I made my family get into the car. We were in the pub car park.

'I'm going in the pub now,' I said to Sue firmly, 'I'll bring you and the kids something out.'

They sat in our car and I went in the pub and ordered myself a whisky and Sue and the kids lemonade and crisps. Sue had stopped drinking; she was too fed up of my drinking. I took the lemonade and crisps out on a tray and handed them round.

'I'll be back later, tuck into this,' I said casually. For an hour and a half they sat in the car park until I appeared well-satisfied with the booze I had consumed. I was not quite so worried about Sue as she looked healthy and so some of my early protectiveness had slipped.

The thought of her death was being pushed farther and farther to the back of my mind. I climbed into the car and drove off the worse for drink. If I had been stopped by the police I would never has passed the Breathalyser test.

I never cared that the kids saw me drunk. Nothing had to interfere with my life. I had already made my mind up I would go regularly to church and I didn't mind if Sue and the kids came along. On the Sunday mornings I left them in the pub car park after church and went drinking. It was the only part of Sunday Sue didn't enjoy! She always wanted to go straight home, but I would never let her. The kids were bored, but it didn't bother me. All four of them enjoyed church services, but they hated the car park.

Three or four weeks after I had begun going to church the pastor announced there was going to be a baptism on the following Sunday evening. I knew the man who was to be baptised and I decided out of curiosity that we would all go along that evening. The church was packed to the doors. I sat rooted to my seat scanning the members of the congregation.

The water where he was to be baptised was cordoned off with a rope and a crowd gathered as he went towards the pool, dressed in a loose fitting robe. Reg spoke audibly and sincerely on what it meant to be a follower of Christ.

'Jesus has died for you on the cross of Calvary. He wants you to give your life to Him.'

He spoke to the whole church who listened in silence, but for me it was as if he spoke only to me. His words penetrated, 'God so loved the world that he *gave* his only begotten Son, that whoever believes in him should not perish but have everlasting life' (John 3:16).

As the man went under the water and came up, the congregation burst into joyful singing. A strange confusing turmoil was racing through me. I whispered to Sue, 'Come with me. I want to talk to someone.'

At the close of the service I sat with Ed, an elder of the church. I gave my life to Christ and prayed with faith. I knew only a greater sense of peace afterwards. I became a Christian then but I began to live a double life.

Immediately Sue and I wanted to be baptised together. The pastor agreed to baptise us and we went along to classes. We didn't know much but we enjoyed learning.

We were baptised at the end of May 1978. As we went down into the water and came up we could see Christine and Carol cheering. Everyone was very happy and it was a tremendous service. Sue's brothers came along for the baptism. The verse we were given was 'If anyone is in Christ, he is a new creation' (2 Corinthians 5:17). Gradually I was getting a glimmer of what faith was all about and with it came a greater assurance that Sue was definitely healed.

It all came over a long period of time. My baptism over, I attended church regularly, often drunk. My bloodshot eyes and the smell of whisky mixed with lager on my breath gave me away, although I prided myself on being able to hold my liquor. I still had the sneaking conviction that the people and the pastor were secret drinkers. I didn't bother hiding my drinking. I used to watch the pastor waving his arms to make his points and singing the choruses enthusiastically. No one who hadn't been drinking would act like that.

I had some strange experiences in church. As I was sitting there listening to the pastor's sermons I couldn't help glancing around me wondering if people were staring at me. I moved uncomfortably as I thought that the pastor was talking about me. Everything he said week by week seemed to apply to Sue and me. It wasn't just my experience but Sue felt it also. We couldn't go to church without hearing something which privately seemed to belong to our situation. I felt at times as if I was in the hot seat!

I was beginning to realise there was another person around and that was the devil. I spent my time agreeing with his whispers.

'Look, George, enjoy yourself in church but don't go overboard. You've got to keep up your social life. You don't need to stop drinking, God doesn't expect you to give up your enjoyment. Keep your friends, be happy with your wife and the kids, and have a good time as well.'

The devil was so persuasive I never got round to disagreeing with him, either in church or at home. If I had a nagging doubt when a person at church would tactfully try to point out that you shouldn't be constantly under the influence when you came to church, his suave, seemingly sincere voice had an impact.

I even boasted to Christine, 'If God's around when I'm drinking, I could drink the whole pub up and remain sober.'

I used God for my own purposes and what I sowed I went out to reap. I couldn't kick the seven-day-a-week habit. I couldn't admit that to anyone, not even myself. I started drinking two bottles of spirits a day, but that wasn't enough, and so I drank lager also.

Money disappeared as I drank. I couldn't see Sue's suffering and the kids' lack of a stable home life in the midst of my alcoholic haze.

A doctor in the church fellowship told me I was ruining my health and that it wasn't God's will for my life. I still avoided the woman who had spoken the words when Sue was in hospital about God using me. I wasn't embarrassed – how could I be – my drinking was for relaxation.

On Sunday evenings I went in the pub after church and came out at closing time. I went round to the pastor's house and banged on the door.

'Let me in, I've got to see you. The devil's after me. You've got to deliver me.'

Reg and his wife Sylvia talked to me for hours. On Saturday evenings I would turn up at mid-night or one o'clock in the morning. Sylvia used to phone up Sue and say, 'Don't worry Sue, George has turned up here. We'll send him home as soon as we can.'

I established a pattern that lasted two years. I was a regular caller at the manse and they knew it was me when the knocker went late at night. Sue became more and more frustrated. I kept on going to church each week. I wanted Christianity but I wanted to keep my old social life as well. My awareness of being a Christian was acute, but to many I must have seemed the worse kind of hypocrite.

Over that two years Sue never saw me unless I was pie-eyed with drink. Every morning I got up and was sick in the toilet and to my horror blood came up from my stomach. I tried to forget about it but every morning it was the same: blood was mixed with my vomit. Besides church every Sunday we had joined a local housegroup and as often as I could I went along with Sue and the kids. One evening I left early taking the kids with me. Sue remained behind talking to the group, but she eventually began to weep. She felt she couldn't cope with my drinking, our debts were piling up and we couldn't pay the mortgage. She was waiting any day to be made homeless on the streets with the kids.

'I can't take any more. For the sake of the kids I'm going to have to leave George,' Sue said sadly.

The leader of the group phoned the pastor and arranged for Sue to go up and see him. Sue saw Reg and Sylvia but Reg's words though kind, couldn't comfort her.

'Sue, I can't help you by yourself. I'm going to have to see you both together. Bring George up here to see me and I will try again to talk with him.'

When I was in a drunken stupor Sue told me.

'The Lord has told me that if you don't give up

drink now, I've got to leave you.'

She spoke without emotion and calmly. My reactions were instantaneous. I went into shock. How could Sue, who had gone through so much with me and whom I loved with all my heart, think of leaving me? I couldn't cope with it and immediately wanted another drink. The following day Sue approached me about seeing Reg, 'I'm not going to see the Gestapo,' I said sullenly.

Sue argued with me and I ended up phoning Reg to say, 'My car's broken down I won't be able to come.'

'That's all right, George, I can come down to see you at your house,' Reg said happily.

'No, don't do that,' I interrupted him hastily, 'If I'm coming I'll make it to you.' I put the phone down and made for the pub. My mood got better the more I drank. Sue came in during the evening to get me. I would't budge. 'I am not going up to the Gestapo so leave me alone, will you, woman.'

'George, I'm not leaving you alone. I want you to take this opportunity to save our marriage.' Sue's voice sounded strained as she spoke. I began arguing with her, but in the end to please her I went up to the manse.

Reg and Sylvia showed Sue and I into the study. I sat on a leather chair with wooden curved arms. I was filled with rebellion and said defiantly, 'I want to leave here by 10.30, so I can get a drink before the pubs shut.'

They were praying in tongues. I was thinking, 'Here we are at Christmas time, my birthday's coming up and there's the neighbours' social, so the quicker I get out of here the better! I'm not going to give up drink.' Nobody was talking to me, I just sat in the chair, drunk, dishevelled and defiant.

A voice spoke to me, 'George, won't you admit to me you are an alcoholic?' I knew it was the Lord and I said, 'No, Lord I can't do that.' The Lord's voice spoke more insistently to me then, 'George, admit to me you are an alcoholic.'

I broke down and groaned, 'Lord forgive me, I am.' Instantaneously I sobered up, my head felt as if it opened up and a hundred-ton weight was being lifted out. I could feel myself almost rising in the chair. I stood up with a flowing sensation moving through me and I turned to Sue and said, 'That's it Sue, I am never going to drink again.'

Reg told me, 'George you don't need deliverance, you need to use your will and turn it over to God. He will cure you.'

I was completely sober and I couldn't remember the last time I had been. We were able then to all talk freely.

Reg cautioned me, 'George, you will never be able to take even one sip of drink ever again.'

'I know that and don't worry I won't,' I said smiling and relieved, it was so good to be without a fuzzy head!

As Sue and I left, Sylvia stopped us, 'Sue and George, I haven't said anything to Reg but how about you and the family coming and spending Boxing Day with us? You agree, don't you Reg?'

Yes, we would both be very pleased if you could come.'

I was astounded because running through my mind had been the thought of all the neighbours inviting us round for a drink. It was the worst drinking day of the year for me.

Looking at Sue and smiling I said, 'Sue and I will be glad to come. You have just solved a problem for me.' In that moment I knew Jesus was going to help me through all the difficulties.

We went home to bed, and I awoke clear-headed and didn't rush to the bathroom. I wasn't sick and I was sober too! I bent over Sue in the bed.

'Sue, Jesus has healed me!' God had kept us both together and now we were whole people able to face the world.

7 *A debt to pay!*

George's story continues...

Stone-cold sober, I went to work filled with zeal and determined to do my best. Throughout the day I didn't move from the yard. I stood there, my helmet covering my brown hair, and goggles placed strategically over my eyes, wielding my blow torch. I stopped for breaks and moved into the small canteen, where I consumed cups of coffee to give me energy. At lunch time I pulled out my wad of sandwiches. Thick slices of white bread with cheese and pickle wedged in between. I had become a contented man. I didn't say anything to the men who were working with me but I saw them glancing furtively at me and smothering a laugh occasionally. It wasn't bothering me that they thought of me as the absentee boss. I went through the day whistling a tune and perfectly happy.

On the second day I did the same as the first. I caught the men making bets on how long I would last, which just made me smile! The third and the fourth day one of them tried to lace my coffee with whisky. I went into the canteen and picked up the coffee off the counter and was about to drink it when the unmistakable smell of alcohol drifted into my nostrils. Feeling slightly sick I chucked it away. The victim had been delivered from that particular demon! After it happened twice the men left me alone although some of them must have been richer in their pockets!

I hadn't a clue as to the extent of my debts and so soberly facing up to reality shocked my system. I had torn up the bills that lay on our mat by the front door. It was obvious they were demands because I saw them outlined in red through the envelopes. I didn't bother reading them, I was confident if I tore them up they would go away.

Sue had tried to tell me, 'George, we've got to pay them. The mortgage is in arrears and we'll be evicted.'

I had ignored her before but now without hitting the bottle again I would have to face the facts. At home in the evening I groaned as the bills, which were no longer torn up, lay before me on the living-room table. Unhappy and miserable, the amounts of money owing reached astronomical proportions. I closed my eyes. Trembling and panicking I wanted to run out of the house and leave everything behind. The bank manager had written and closed my account. It had been terribly overdrawn. I had at the time been pleased to get the money into my hands and pass it on to the owner of the local pub. Sue had cleverly wheedled some money out of me occasionally to cover the odd bill and the shopping, but the vast majority of the bills was arrayed before me, in full view. The fool was looking at his ruin. The harvest had been reaped from the past. I didn't know what to do and so I calculated how much money I owed quickly; £4000. The figure stared up at me from the scrawling notes. I checked again and sighed in despair. No, I couldn't change the figure.

I went to church on the Sunday morning taking the burden with me. Miserable and uncertain I didn't feel my usual cocky self. The muscles on my arms and chest hadn't made me feel like a man. I was a worm and no man. Sue urged me to talk it over with Reg.

'I am sure he can help you sort out this mess,' she said, worried but assured at the same time.

Reg led me into the study again and I poured out the total sum of my problems to him. I finished by saying,

'There's just no way out, Reg. I've lost everything, the house and my business are in a shambles. It's all happening just when we had a new start.'

Reg's calmness and concern flowed out towards me as I sat in the chair, 'George, do you believe that the Lord has healed you from drink?'

There was just no way I could say no to that question. Every Friday, Reg rang me to ask how my week had gone. He and I both knew I was a free man.

'Reg, yes of course I know that,' my voice must have sounded puzzled at his seemingly irrelevant question.

'Well then, do you believe the Lord can take away your debt?'

Reg's penetrating sympathetic eyes held a look of enquiry. I shuffled uncomfortably in the hard seat, pausing to think, and a silence fell between us.

Reluctantly, I struggled with the answer he was expecting to hear and what I couldn't evade I definitely stated.

'Yes, Reg, I do believe the Lord can take away my debt.' The bondage of doubt, uncertainty and hopelessness was gone in that instance. There was nothing left to talk about, we only bowed united before the Lord, pleading with Him to help me sort out the chaos I had caused. Released from pressure, I rose from the chair and took Reg's hand.

'Thanks for your help. I know now I can make it, the Lord and me will sort the whole thing out.' I went home confident and expectant even though it needed another miracle to happen.

'I've just brought in another load, George,' one of the men remarked the following day. I could look around at the mounting piles of metal. Old railway lines, scrap cars, pieces of metal in huge mounds were gathered. Rusty and exposed to the weather, my work was expanding before my eyes. The loads kept on being driven in by the men. There was more work and my business was prospering and as I began to expand more men found work with me. At home I would gather four bills out of the pile remarking to Sue, 'I think I can settle these now.'

The contracts for work were increasing and as the money came in my bills were all met. I saw my debts dissolved within three months. I saw the unexpected happen. As I prayed, the Lord brought me more business and within three months I didn't have one debt left. £4000 in arrears had disappeared as if it had never been! I was able to give the glory to God. My miracle had happened and it was as if I was an observer looking in at the pool of God's resources. Prayer had been answered and chaos turned into order. With God blessing my business, I felt I could afford to be generous. From putting ten pence a week into the offering I would carelessly throw in a tenner. I was satisfied I was being generous enough. Sue and I began to enjoy again the money that was coming in. The mortgage was once more being paid and we could afford not only to buy as much food as we wanted but also to eat in the best restaurants in town. Our tatty worn-out furniture we started to replace and Sue indulged in a whole new wardrobe. We planned the best holidays we could think of. God was blessing me and my business. We were rich people abundantly provided for, but things began to go wrong in a way which was frustrating and bewildering.

I used to pray for every contract I got and I was landing quite a few jobs which I felt were an answer to prayer. I saw God as repaying the suffering I had caused myself and Sue. The jobs I got were plenty, but the ones I actually kept became fewer. Something seemed to go wrong with many of the contracts. I would almost land them then they left like the fish that got away. A big one was lost as quickly as I gained it. I was praying, happy I had enough to live on, but work was gradually becoming more difficult. My faith was still there, but I was getting a bit worried.

When I answered the phone and heard the man at the other end offering me a large contract in Avon-mouth, I jumped at it and dreamed of a holiday in the sun. I had a cheap banger and I set off one Saturday morning with the pastor's son and a good mate of mine, Vic, who was thinking of joining me in the scrap-metal business. It was a clear day and we

were making good progress on the motorway to
Avonmouth. But it didn't last long. The car had a
puncture and we had to stop and change the front
tyre. It delayed us half an hour and as we set off again
with a splutter, the car died on us. The engine had
packed up and we were well and truly broken down.
The day passed on the motorway and we returned
eventually to Swindon without ever having reached
Avonmouth. I was apologetic so I phoned the manse
and Sylvia answered, 'I am awfully sorry Malcom's
had a wasted day with me, and we are back so late.'

Sylvia's clear resonant tones came over the line.

'That's all right, George. Do you think the Lord's
trying to tell you something through this?'

Impatiently, I replied, 'I don't know what it can
be at all. It was a confounded waste of a day.'

Soon after that I rang off. The Lord surely hadn't
anything to say to me because of an accident.

On Sunday morning the family all dressed up, we
went to church. It was our weekly tonic and a chance
to understand the Bible better. It was a struggle for
me to understand my Bible. That Sunday morning,
Reg preached on tithing. I was douched in a bucket
of cold water. He spoke about giving a tenth of what
you earned to the Lord, and I knew that in church I
had unexpectedly found out the reason why so many
of my jobs were falling by the wayside. I had never
heard about tithing before but it was what I needed
to do. The solution was dynamic. My fantastic tenner
was a mockery of what I actually earned. Flashing
through my mind flew the money I had realised in
just a week.

Waiting until I got home excited, I went into

detail. At first I took just the figures for the previous week. The shock of the figure in front of me halted my enthusiasm.

I began a conversation with God,

'If I give you all that I'll be no better off then I have been in the past.'

The inner voice responded to my dilemma with firmness. 'George, you can't afford not to give it to me.'

I looked in dismay at the startling revelation I held in my hand and it was without conviction and hesitatingly that I made my final decision, 'All right, Lord, I will try it for a few weeks but if it doesn't work and I don't see how it can, I am going to feel free to stop.'

Tithing began a new chapter in my life and my relationship with the Lord deepened. I could never end my tithing because God taught me in that few weeks the truth that He was the provider for me – and all that I now possessed He had given to me. The Lord was no man's debtor, there was no lack. My tithing experiment became a way of life. A further step was needed and warily and slowly I made my decision after much prayer.

I had never been a business tycoon and every contract I had to pray for at first, but now it had reached a stage where I had so many jobs it was a matter of picking and choosing. On my own I was a walking catastrophe guaranteed to be a failure. It was common for me to pray for the Lord's guidance as to which contract to take. When I felt it was right to go ahead things ran smoothly. I only made mistakes when I didn't ask God. With the months of learning came wisdom and eventually a pact with my Maker. I handed over my rights and my business to the One who was really in charge and whose decisions would always be right. Any double-dealing was over, for God wanted my business as well as me. He became the Owner and gave me the place of the manager.

It was good actually to have done something. There was no way to regret it after. I relaxed as the work expanded and more men were taken on, including my son Tony, as he left school.

We went as a family to church. The congregation was getting bigger, a few visitors were scattered around, curious as rumours about Rodbourne Baptist grew. The ministry given included prayer for people's healing and counsel for those who came in distress. Services sparked off requests for help. People prayed with those who came forward with great eagerness. I wasn't now plagued by unbelief but there was one thing which I saw in the services which filled me with scepticism. Men and women used to go out to the front and one of the elders would rest their hands on their heads. They would pray over them, sometimes in English and at other times in tongues. It was extraordinary to watch that person who had been standing perfectly erect suddenly keel over and be laid out flat on the floor for a few minutes.

I whispered to Sue, 'I am not going forward and even if I did there is no way that I would fall down like that. It just can't be right.' I had learned to live with nagging pains in my back, after all, I did strenuous labouring work. It was uncomfortable and at times difficult to live with but I accepted it. They had been with me a few years but on one Sunday evening I gave in to the Lord's promptings, I whispered to Sue that I was going forward and I had a chat to God.

'Lord I'm going forward about these pains in my back, because I want prayer for healing. I want to be healed and to fall down, but I am going to resist the falling down.'

After my bargaining with God I stepped out to the front and waited for the approaching man to reach me.

'What would you like prayer for George?' he asked seriously and intently.

'I need prayer to heal the pains in my back,' I said confidently.

I closed my eyes consciously to resist the falling down. He began to pray and the next minute I found myself flat out on the floor. I opened my eyes in surprise and pulled myself into a sitting position. I felt warm and comforted.

As I stood on my feet, realisation that the pains had left my back flooded into me. Exhilarated and a trifle ashamed, I sat down next to Sue and whispered in her ear, 'You know Sue, it is really real that falling down, you can't stop it!'

Sue who had never doubted it, just smiled smugly at me.

God must have had quite a chuckle at me. The bargainer got more of a bargain than he imagined! The Holy Spirit was certainly around today. I wondered what He would do next for me.

PART TWO

RECLAIMED FOR GOD'S PURPOSES

8   *The dove and the olive*

George's story continues...

I learnt more about the Holy Spirit and began to partake rather than stare in amazement at what was happening to people around me. Sue and I both developed the gift of tongues which helped us to pray and worship the Lord. We were slowly but surely experiencing what it meant to walk in the power of the Holy Spirit. We didn't have a dramatic second encounter with the Holy Spirit but nevertheless the assurance of His presence grew until we excitedly waited to see what else the Holy Spirit had in store for us. In worship we learned to relax in God's wonderful presence. That presence became fullness of joy. The newest and most precious experience we gained was peace. Peace that dissolved the disorder, the anger and fears of the past.

It was Reg and Sylvia who invited us to our first Full Gospel Businessmen's meal in 1981. The three-course roast dinner was held in a Saturday evening in a ballroom at the Goddard Arms Restaurant. Listening to the testimony that evening brought home to me the need to tell others that Jesus wanted them to give their lives to Him. I had been selfish in another way – what I had been given I hadn't willingly shared with others. At the close of the meeting some went forward seeking salvation and I had something to think about. Going along a couple of times convinced me of my need for fuller involvement and I decided to become a member of the Swindon Full Gospel Business Men's Chapter. Ted Nichols, the local Business Men's President, explained the beginnings of this clear movement of God's Holy Spirit.

'The Swindon Chapter began last year. I went along to a Bristol meeting where I saw people who would never go into a church, go forward to accept Jesus into their lives. After reading *The Happiest People on Earth*, the story of the founder of the Full Gospel Business Men's Fellowship, I felt I could identify with their aims. I caught the vision of ordinary people coming to know Jesus as their personal Saviour, and employer and employee meeting together before the Lord on equal terms. We never preach sermons but always someone will give a testimony. It is their personal story of how God touched their lives. The plumber relates to the plumber and the teacher to the teacher. There are two kinds of miracles we see here. The first and most important miracle is salvation and the second one which is an added bonus is people's healing. It is our desire to reach people while there is time and win men particularly for the kingdom of God.'

I was fired with enthusiasm and vision, enjoying the meetings with different Christians from many churches in the Swindon area. At first I would only take people from my church fellowship along to the dinners but soon I was taking up to ten people to the evening rallies, and also to the Saturday breakfasts.

The Full Gospel Business Men's Fellowship had been going about six months, when I joined. The men held prayer meetings every Thursday in one of the member's houses. There were only about twelve of us meeting together regularly but more were joining. It was definitely small beginnings! I had gone along with Vic, who had started work with me after being a lorry driver. He had only recently become a Christian although his wife had been a Christian for a few years. Before his conversion, he had been a tough character, but God had dealt with him as firmly as he had dealt with me. At one of the dinners he had had prayer for healing and God had answered. We became firm friends and joined the group that met together for prayer each week.

The Lord let me into praying and believing in Him to answer. I prayed with men with open hearts, whose lives were at God's disposal. Their hearts were inflamed with fire from God. Our prayers would rise up until late evening and it was a blessing just to share together in the future work God wanted to do in Swindon. I got to the stage where I could believe God for something bigger.

One evening we were round at Ted's house. As a group there was a discouraged atmosphere and prayer wasn't coming easily. Only thirty to forty men and women were expected to come along to the next meal, held at our usual venue, and we all wanted many more. There was only one solution to that problem: we had to pray them in, I thought.

I began praying quietly then out loud, 'Lord, you see that our numbers for the dinner are only about forty. Lord, we want to see people coming along, believing and being saved. Lord, send us double that number, making it eighty people. We want to see your name lifted up and glorified.'

Excited and exhilarated I paused then and looked around at the other men who had joined in by saying a loud Amen! as I finished.

Suddenly the phone rang and Ted answered it and shouted, 'I've got another booking.' During that evening the bookings continued to come in and by the time we went home to bed, we had seventy definitely coming to the dinner. God did the roll call after all!

I had taken on several men to work with me collecting and cutting up the scrap metal. Some were Christians; some weren't. I was cautious however, because I didn't want to pressurise anyone into becoming a Christian. God would have to do the converting! I made no secret of my faith but also tried to treat all my workers fairly and equally.

I got the opportunity to talk to a man whom I had known quite a while. He was quite a nice-looking, young, dark-haired man who had a Catholic upbringing but had lapsed from the faith. In a rest period he was talking to me when he said unexpectedly, 'George, you've changed that much over the years I've known you. What's the reason for it?'

He had seen me when I was a drunken so and so and in a mess and so when I began talking about Jesus he listened attentively.

'God has done so much for me. He changed my life and he is interested in you and wants to give you a fresh start.' My words didn't make him turn away or give a hurried excuse to leave.

'He certainly seems to have done something for you,' he remarked with casual interest. I took him up on his words.

'I tell you what, if you'd like to know more about it, come along with Sue and me to a Full Gospel Business Men's Dinner. You'll find out that it's not only me God has helped!'

'O.K.,' he said with a grin, 'I think I wouldn't mind going.' It was time to be getting on with the job so I quickly said,

'It's this coming Monday evening, we'll give you a lift.'

The testimony on the Monday evening when he came along made such an impact on Kevin Reynolds that it was almost inevitable that when they asked people to come out the front who wanted to know about Jesus and give their lives to Him, he should be the first one out there. Another person was brought into the kingdom of God and the angels were probably doing some rejoicing then! I was just God's link in the chain and only in a very superficial way had I been involved, for he had made his transaction with God, who had been seeking him anyway.

Paying for my guests to come to the dinner was for me a love offering to the Lord. Sometimes it cost me something to give that amount of money but God always repaid me. My work continued to flourish and there was just no way I could outgive God. That was impossible, the flow of money coming in showed me that.

Sue was always busy telling people what God had done for her. Chloe and her now conducted friendly discussions in the garden. God's love disintegrated the hate between them. One recognised that, the

other didn't. Sue was finding it easy to discuss any
subject with Chloe and she was closer to Chloe than
anyone else in the Close. Chloe by this time had
found the reality of Sue's healing as five years had
passed and Sue wasn't in her coffin. She was still
abounding with glowing health. I had just been
appointed to the Executive of the Full Gospel
Business Men's Swindon Chapter, when I was talking
to Sue one evening, while we were watching some
television.

'Sue, just pop around to next door and see if Chloe
and Steven would like a night out with us. We could
take them to the dinner.'

Sue tidied herself up and after smoothing down
her dress, she went across the grass patch in front of
our house and knocked on their door. She came back
a few minutes later, happy and smiling.

'They both agreed to come with us, George.'

We arranged to take them to a Saturday morning
breakfast. It was always a good meal and full up we
relaxed and listened as the speaker who as usual was
a man, spoke for about forty minutes, sharing his
experience in life and how he had found Christ to be
all he needed. The power of the Holy Spirit and the
sense of the Lord's presence were all around us.
There was a general anointing and people left their
seats eagerly to get to the front table.

Sue and I had hoped, but had been uncertain as to
the reaction of our neighbours. Sue glanced at Chloe
beside her and noticed the tears pouring down her
cheeks. She rose and whispered to Sue, 'I'm going
forward.' Steven too had obviously been moved
because he left his seat and went out together with
Chloe to speak to the men who were waiting to

minister. Sue and I sat praying for them and thanking the Lord for their response. On the Sunday morning we all went together to church. Their son Paul had been going to Covenanters and he was later baptised.

Love is God, and He is the One who dispenses it to all who want it. Nobody escapes His notice or concern. Our neighbours were as important to Him as we were. Love wins over hate.

Indifference seemed to be the only response from most of our family, which was disappointing but we had to accept it. Sue, my sister, verged on the critical side, but I was really pleased when she agreed to come to one of the dinners with Sue and me. That evening she accepted Jesus into her life and over the next few months my mother commented on the change in her.

I was always eager for the Lord to reach into my mother's life and was desperate to know that she would be going to heaven with us. My mother was the best mother in the world and she had as a child been in Sunday School. She was respectable and clean-living and respected God at a distance. The idea of a personal relationship with God didn't seem important to her. She listened without understanding Sue and me. When we asked her to come to a London rally of Crusade for World Revival one weekend she came willingly. My mother had one major problem, she was hard of hearing and wore a hearing aid, which she occasionally fiddled with. The meeting was filled with praise and the message was for people to find God. As evidence of their desire to know God, they wanted people to stand.

I whispered to Mum, 'Stand up,' and she slowly

rose to her feet.

Afterwards, bewildered, she asked me, 'George, why did you want me to stand up?' I realised then she hadn't dedicated her life to the Lord. It was a disappointing moment and I had made a mistake. In my eagerness, I had tried to push her into the kingdom of God and no one gets there that way! A few weeks later Mum became seriously ill and I was really worried. Sue and a friend went round when I couldn't go to visit her. With ease and assurance of the Lord's guidance there, while she was lying down, she asked Jesus into her life and God showed that He could take all mistakes and use them to filfil His purposes. My mother was like a flower that opened of its own accord in the sun. She showed then the beauty of salvation in her own life.

We were the fingers on the body of Christ reaching out into the world. Each week we shared in church worship and on Sunday evening Sue found herself becoming more distracted as she went. She would sit next to one of the teenagers. It was obvious that church wasn't meeting all their needs. Their attention wandered and they didn't seem to be participating in the services. She became very troubled. She took the problem to the Lord.

In a quiet time she felt the Lord saying, 'I want you to work with young people and to provide them with a place to go.'

After praying she jotted down on paper points she felt would be needed to be looked into. She told me when I appeared in a good mood. I stared at her, as if she had gone mad, responding indignantly, 'Sue, haven't you enough to do looking after four kids of your own, without lumbering us with other peoples'?'

She just laid out on the coffee table the notes she had made and carried on talking, but by the end of our discussion I had relented. The Lord showed both of us that it was His will in different ways. It was all right having an idea, but we hadn't even asked the young people at the church whether it was what they wanted. They didn't really know us but as it was Tony's birthday on the Sunday we invited a few of them home for the party.

Laying the plan before them we awaited their response.

'I'd like to bring records.'

'It would be good to be able to play games.'

'Let's have a tuck shop.'

Sue sat there ticking away at the list she had made during her quiet time. By the time all of them had had their say, there wasn't an item on it that hadn't been marked against! God was leading us to do a practical thing and it didn't look as if it was going to be too spiritual either! It was good however to feel His blessing and God intervened when we found a building we wanted to use as a youth group centre.

A community centre was about the most obvious place for the youth group to meet so we went along there and the lady who met us was far from encouraging. She was a portly caretaker with a cigarette hanging out of her mouth.

'You'll have to ask the Council,' she said abruptly, 'Myself, I think you're wasting your time. We've just got rid of one youth group. Wrecked the place they did. Come along and I'll show you.'

She showed us into the room. There were displays

of crude art and carved initials all around. Our hearts sank and we politely told her we would apply.

Drafting a letter to the Council was difficult. All we could say seemed very feeble; we were a church youth group and a private organisation, and would take care of the building. Far from satisfied I posted it.

The letter which arrived on my mat from the Council was a surprise. The Council unanimously voted us the use of the building. We had our club on Thursday evenings! A minor miracle perhaps, but one of the steps when God showed us we were doing His will.

The next step was the approval of the church leadership. We approached the elders who promised to take the matter up with church.

We went along, but looking around at the members present, we noticed most of them were a long way past the youth-club age group. Gloomily, we waited for the negative reactions.

The first to rise to his feet after the motion was put to the meeting, was a white-haired elderly gentleman. His words were a relief, 'There was a youth club here a few years ago. I think this is a good idea.' Having given his opinion he sat down quickly. A lady, also elderly, followed him and she too had gone along to a youth club at one time. Astonished, Sue and I found that there was no opposition to begin the youth group and even the fact that it wasn't on church ground was ignored. The youth group was born!

My commitment to the young people became important to me. More youngsters joined me and we were realising what a task it was, when gradually I became aware of the conflict of interests. I was Vice

President of the Full Gospel Businenss Men's Fellowship and the Thursday prayer meetings clashed with the youth club. The need of the young people was great and there was also my concern for the work of the Swindon Chapter of the Full Gospel Business Men's Fellowship. I was driven to prayer about which was to be my priority. God spoke to me in a quiet time, early one morning, 'George, I want you to look after the young people and give them your time.'

After clearly hearing His voice, I had little choice but to resign from being Vice President. I decided to continue as a member and bring people along to the meetings, but from then on, the young people took first place in our order of priorities. Sue and I gained from our contact with them.

What was a job of work became lots of fun!

9 *The seal of guarantee*

Sue's story...

George and I didn't attend one of the Full Gospel Business Men's breakfasts and so Sylvia lent me the tape of the meeting. The speaker was a German who had been given a vision from the Lord to hold a conference in Berlin to be called, 'Jesus in Berlin.'

Sylvia commented as she gave me the tape, 'I feel the Lord wants me to go to that conference.'

As I listened to the German speaking I felt an overwhelming certainty that the Lord wanted me there also. Without saying anything to George, I handed him the tape.

He played it and said, 'That's quite a good tape, I think we'll play it to the youth group.'

'Didn't you feel you should be going?' I said hopefully and rather anxiously.

'No, I don't think I'm meant to be going, but if you think you want to go I won't hinder you,' George said disinterestedly.

Disappointed, I went along to the youth group and there we played the tape. Twelve of them wanted to go to Berlin! I talked with Sylvia and we decided to organise a party. Only one other adult, a lady called Pat, who had recently been widowed, felt she wanted to go. We sent for details and the young people, Sylvia and I were booked into a school. Pat had been booked into bed and breakfast. This bothered me, that she should be on her own just after losing her husband, so in the end it was arranged that both she and I would share the bed and breakfast accommodation. The conference was to be held at the Olympic Stadium in Berlin. I checked my passport which was a yearly one and noticed it said West Berlin on it and so didn't think any more about it, until it came time to show the organiser of the trip our documents.

'You can't travel on this, we are passing through East Germany and there it isn't valid,' he remarked kindly. It was just over two weeks until we were due to leave. I hurriedly sent off to the Newport passport office. I heard nothing. One evening I had a call from a member of the church whose two sons were going on the trip.

'Sue, are you going down to Newport to pick up your passport?' Harold remarked, 'I've had a telephone call that Brad and Brendon's passport is ready.'

'Yes, I've been thinking of going as this postal strike is on,' I remarked, I'll just ask George if he can take me.'

'George,' I yelled, 'Can you take me over to Newport to collect my passport?'

'Yes, that should be all right,' he called back.

'I'll pick it up for you, just drop me in a letter authorising me to collect it,' I finished off before putting down the telephone. The trip to Newport was a bit of a nuisance, but with George taking me I was happy about it. My car was a wreck and I could only just turn a corner in it.

All the arrangements were going so smoothly that when George phoned from work to say he couldn't take me and I would have to get a taxi, I exploded.

'What! All that money to pick up a passport? It doesn't seem worth it!' George in his pragmatic way just brushed aside what I said, 'Can't be helped, have a good trip.'

When the taxi came it was going to be £20 and the taxi driver remarked as we pulled up outside the Newport office, 'It will be £2 an hour waiting time.'

Annoyed, I thought I wouldn't be five minutes in there! I took the lift up to the first floor and entered a huge room and then stopped in dismay. The benches were crowded with people and all around the walls and over most of the floor space people were queuing and waiting to reach a large counter. I thought gloomily of the taxi driver waiting outside. I thought I was going to be there all day. Gazing at the people and past them, I noticed in the corner of the room a small alcove with a counter. There was nobody standing there. I pushed my way past the men and women who made me a channel through to the empty counter. A woman in glasses looked up from her writing and saw me standing there.

'I've come for these passports,' I pushed the letter of authorisation at her. She read it carefully. I carried on talking hurriedly. 'I would also like my own passport.'

'Give me your name and address. I suppose you have been notified by our office that your passport is ready,' she said.

I told her my details and ended hesitantly, 'No, I

haven't been notified. I'm going in two weeks and I need my passport in a hurry.'

She was very firm when she replied, 'I'm sorry, but you won't be able to pick it up straight away. Your friends' passports will be downstairs.' She bent down over her work and I turned away towards the crowd and began making my way towards the door. Soon I was entering a room where the queue was much smaller. A man standing in front of me smiled and I ventured to ask him.

'Did you get notified that your passport was ready?'

'Yes, I did, they won't issue one unless you are notified.'

Another lady in the queue turned round and answered, 'I was also notified.' I tried someone behind me and she also had been notified. As the queue gradually receded I became more and more depressed. It didn't look as if I would be going to Berlin and I had had a very expensive trip, which had been a waste of time. The man at the desk took the letter I held and a few minutes later brought back the passports.

Desperately, I said to him, 'You wouldn't happen to know if my passport is ready? I haven't been notified.' I gave him my name and address.

'It seems unlikely, but I will go and check for you anyway, just wait a minute.' After speaking, he got up from the desk and disappeared into an interior room. I couldn't see what was happening and waited impatiently for him to re-appear. He came back with an impassive look on his face, 'Mrs Hayes, your passport is upstairs if you would like to collect it.'

'Would I!' I said, breathless with excitement, leaving him hurriedly and making for the exit. Back upstairs the huge room was now overspilling with men, women and children. Daunted, I didn't know what to do next. Hesitating for a few seconds, I went through the crowd once more to the small neglected counter. The same lady sat there working, but on her desk lay a brown envelope. Typed on it was my name and address. 'That letter you have there, it's mine,' I said, pointing at the envelope.

'You can take it,' she said stopping briefly to hand it to me. Quickly I got through the crowd and reached the lift. A lady stepped in with me.

'You must have been in there hours, with all those people. I'm glad I only had to give in a form,' she remarked casually. I glanced at my watch and was surprised.

'No, I have only been here twenty-five minutes.' Amazed and filled with joy I realised then that the Lord was intervening to get me to Berlin. He obviously had a purpose in my going there. The dark taxi was parked close to the office. The cab driver was quite surprised to see me back to quickly.

'You've been gone such a short time, I won't charge you any waiting time,' he observed as I climbed in. I sat back gratefully in the seat as I was glad I had got away from the crowds. Our home journey was uneventful.

George came home with a surprise too: the man who had been the reason that George hadn't been able to take me to Newport had paid for the taxi ride! George was now sure that the Lord wanted me in Berlin.

On the Thursday afternoon, the fifteen from the church gathered where the coach was waiting. Some

Christians from other churches and areas of England joined us. Ours was the only contingent going from England and the fellowship over to Berlin was enjoyable, helping a long trip to pass quickly. We arrived late on the Friday evening and had missed the first meeting. Pat and I found the German-style house close to the Olympic stadium, where we were warmly welcomed by a lady who came from East Berlin but was now resident in the West Berlin sector. The plump jolly lady chatted to us as long as she possibly could. We were both so exhausted that we politely made our excuses to get quickly to bed. We sank into the welcome sheets and thought of the young people roughing it. I gave a sigh of relief.

On the Saturday morning after a breakfast of sausages, we set off for the stadium. There was a crowd of thirty thousand gathered to listen. As the morning progressed, I became irritated by the German translated into English. Bored by lunch time, Pat and I decided to skip the afternoon meeting and come back for the evening session. We wandered around the beautiful city of Berlin fascinated by what we saw. We also ate well, arriving back at the stadium in time for the meeting. The meeting was so like the morning meeting that I yawned my way through it. By this time I was feeling disillusioned, the fellowship had been good, the scenery illuminating, but what was God wanting me in Berlin for? As the evening wore on and we made our way back to our comfortable lodgings I became under the impression that I had somehow failed God. He had wanted me to see something and I hadn't been looking in the right direction. Unhappy, I fell asleep.

I awoke at first light and reflected that it was

unusual for me to be roused that early. I was then filled with a great urgency – knowing I had to get to the next meeting.

I shook Pat awake and she stirred slowly, 'We mustn't be late, for some reason I have got to make the next meeting.' We both began to get ready and after we dressed, descended downstairs to be met by the landlady bearing an enormous breakfast. She was in a mood to talk. That day she was going across the West-East barrier to visit her relatives. She began to tell us her story. It was very interesting and threw insights into a way of life we knew nothing about. She explained the complicated procedures and the rigmarole of entering that communist country. She talked for an hour and by the time she finished we both knew the first session had already begun. Making hurried excuses we ran from the house and at top speed headed into the enormous stadium.

We sat down next to a woman and whispered, 'Have we missed much?'

'We just had a speaker from Ireland talking about the IRA,' she said. I had been clutching my programme as we ran but until then I hadn't glanced at it. I looked down opening it up on my lap. The next session was about the Jews and Israel. I knew nothing about it, but at least felt a spark of interest. Pat and I donned our mackintoshes as dark rain clouds covered the sky. It was getting chilly. A small, dark-haired lady mounted the stage. She was about 4ft 11in but she spoke in a clear, bell-like voice. Her words riveted me to the seat. She spoke of a past where all her family died in the holocaust. Around me and throughout the stadium, tears were trickling down the cheeks of the audience. Her moving, sad story touched all the hearts of those present. My own tears fell freely as the agony of her past and the way she found Jesus to be her Messiah was unfolded in such a personal way that pictures were conjured up in the minds of all of us. The Jewish lady quietly concluded and as she finished, the German organiser of the conference came up on stage and moved towards her. In front of us all they met and embraced. The love of Jesus showed in the overcoming of all barriers. The German and Jew found freedom in Christ's love. I had the answer to my question. This was why God had sent me to Berlin. I hadn't missed out His plan for me. As she finished two Israeli singers sang and then spoke about the meaning of the Feast of Tabernacles and gave an open invitation to all to join them in Jerusalem.

The dark clouds were threatening rain, but as they spoke, a small ray of sunshine penetrated the darkness and lit the platform, resting over the heads of the singers. People began to cheer and praise God as the singer said, 'God is sending His blessing.'

As people cheered, the dark clouds parted and blue sky poured through the opening. The blue sky remained over the stadium but the dark clouds stayed on the outside of the stadium. It poured with rain outside the grounds, but within the stadium sunshine reigned! When we saw this taking place, the people began to cheer and praise God all the more!

A burden for the Jews and Israel came upon me. I knew I wasn't a great evangelist and so thought God would give me something practical to do to help. I left Berlin satisfied and ready for my future work.

At home with George I explained, 'George, I'm

going to do something for Israel.'

'What do you think it is, Sue?' he replied.

Vaguely, I mentioned, 'It might be something to do with finance.'

While I had been in Berlin, Bryn had had his birthday and Vic's wife Margaret had made him a cake. The following morning I was washing up her Tupperware container, the soap bubbles were stuck on it when I heard the Lord speaking to me.

'This is how I want you to help my people Israel. I want you to sell Israeli goods.' I looked at the soapy container and thought I must be crazy. I'm tired and I have been overdoing it. That's not even a very Christian thing, it can't be right. Troubled, I left the sink, wiped my hands on a checked tea towel, left the rest of the dishes and went and sat down heavily in the living room. Unable to forget the words that had gone through my mind, I decided to pray, it seemed the best idea for my dilemma.

'Lord, have I heard you? Do you really want me to sell Israeli goods? I am willing, Lord, but I would like three different confirmations that I'm doing your will. I don't know how to go about it, but I am sure you will show me. Lord, I will need some kind of transport, my car is falling apart.' I thanked the Lord and ended my prayer time.

During the morning I thought I should phone my pastor and share with him what I felt the Lord was showing me. I still inwardly thought that I had gone quite mad.

Without saying anything to anybody I contacted Reg at lunch time. His reaction surprised me.

'Sue, it sounds as if the Lord had told you to do this. I will give you all the help I can.' He gave me a list of Jewish suppliers. God had answered postively through one person. I waited expectantly for His next move. It was a hot week and I spent quite a bit of time in the garden, weeding and mowing the lawn. One morning I was stopped by four of my neighbours. Two I spoke to about the city of Berlin, but the last couple of neighbours came together and dropping their shopping bags on the pavement they stopped for a longer chat. Freely I told them how God had guided me to Berlin and how I felt He was leading me to help the Jews.

'I am going to sell Israeli goods on a party-plan basis,' I told them both.

The neighbour who lived nearest me said, 'If you like and if you do get started on your idea, I will hold a party for you.'

'If you hold a party, Dot, I'll come,' the other neighbour followed her lead. Jubilant, I knew that I had the second kind of confirmation I needed.

The following week was my birthday and George had given me my present in advance. When my birthday came, George handed me a set of keys.

'What are these for?' I asked wonderingly.

'Last week the Lord told me to buy you a new car, so I went out and got it.' George said as I hugged him.

'George, I never told you this, but I asked the Lord that if he wanted me to go around selling Israeli goods, I must have some transport. The Lord through you has provided me with the third lot of confirmation I needed.'

George chuckled and then laughed out loud, 'Sue,' he paused, catching his breath, 'Guess what, the car was owned by a Jew!'

I had all my confirmations but I didn't know how to go about getting the goods and I didn't know what I was supposed to say or do with them. Margaret came round for coffee one Tuesday morning; she had been to choir practice the night before.

'Sue, I put your name down for Prayer for Israel literature. I thought you might like it?' she said smiling.

'Never heard of them, but thanks anyway,' I said as we sat there drinking our coffee.

'I put my own name down and I don't know anything about them, either.' Margaret replied.

Prayer for Israel were very quick in sending through the literature and as I opened the envelope, a piece of paper fell out. It was headed 'Israeli Products Centre'. I read it with growing excitement, 'Would you like to be trained to become a representative selling Israeli goods in Christian's homes? We are organising a party-plan system for selling goods to encourage Christians to help the Jews. If you are interested please contact Israeli Products Centre.' A telephone number was given of a man called Arnold Fox who was himself a Jewish Christian. It was so unbelievable that I sat there staring at the paper without reacting for a few minutes. It wasn't long, however, before I was reaching out for the phone and talking directly to Arnold Fox.

'Israeli Products Centre or IPC is just about to be formed. We haven't even held a party yet. I am just forming it and getting together consultants to sell the goods. At the party we hope to speak about Jewish people and also witness to the Lord.'

We met together as a group of fourteen representatives, initially all of us knowing definitely that God wanted us to do that work. Our plans were soon realised and my Israeli goods were delivered. Perfumes, stones from King Solomon's mines, kitchen equipment and toys were amongst my selection of goods. People began to invite me into their homes to show my goods. Fluently and with confidence I could share about the Christian responsibility to the Jews.

Reading the Bible confirmed my commitment to share with others about God's relationship to Israel. Jeremiah 32:37–41 (RSV) came home to me with a new relevance at that time:

> Behold I will gather them from all the countries to which I drove them back to this place, and I will make them dwell in safety. And they shall be my people and I will be their God. I will give them one heart and one way, that they may fear me for ever, for their own good and the good of their children after them. I will make with them an everlasting covenant, that I will not turn away from doing good to them; and I will put the fear of me in their hearts, that they may not turn from me. I will rejoice in doing them good and I will plant them in this land in faithfulness, with all my heart and all my soul.

It was time for the Christian church to see their responsibility for the Jewish nation. It was to Israel that my eyes turned with longing. George wasn't interested, so I couldn't visit then. The parties increased my contact with Christians and I experienced more and more fellowship as my area widened and interest grew in the work. At one of my first parties I met an old schoolfriend, she had been told I had become a Christian but until she saw and heard me at the party she didn't believe it. My relationship with people became more meaningful and I could also share my testimony.

In church one Sunday morning, a visiting preacher had spoken about the woman with the issue of blood. The story is told in Mark, chapter five. The woman with the issue of blood knew she was healed when she touched the hem of Jesus' garment. She didn't think Jesus would notice but he stopped to challenge the crowd. Afraid, she told him the truth. The preaching wasn't powerful, but the words of the visiting preacher penetrated me. It was as if God was saying, 'Sue, you must tell others what I have done for you.' It was a message that remained with me as I began my ministry. I could easily share my concern for the Jews and tell others my own life story.

I had to learn that Satan doesn't like Christians helping the Jews. The people coming along to the parties were a mixture of Christians and non-Christians. Sometimes I saw the evidence of anti-semitism, but the Lord continued to give me a wonderful joy in my ministry. Much support was given me by my friends. I had a commission, 'Go and sell.' I wasn't paid for my work because God had clearly indicated that I didn't need financial support. He would provide for me through other ways.

I was due to take a party in the week at Stroud, about a forty-minute drive from where I lived. I awoke in the morning to find that my body was plagued with aches and pains. I struggled up out of bed and into the bathroom. I felt no better as I got into the car and began the drive. I felt as if I was about to pass out and was going to turn around and go back home when I felt it would be wrong to do that. I thought I can't let the hostess down, so instead of turning back I began to pray while still at the wheel.

'Lord, give me the strength to get to the hostess's house.' I continued praying as the car travelled along the windy road. Feeling better, I arrived at the village. My hostess had given me instructions that if I got lost I was to ask anyone in the village and they would direct me.

'We are such a small community you won't fail to find the house,' she finished confidently. 'I've been the district nurse here for many years and everyone knows me.'

When I got to the village green I knew I was lost and looked around for the oldest person I could find to ask. An old man with a dog was the only person in sight. I told him the lady's name and address. He didn't respond to her name, but he seemed to know where the house was and I felt I could invite him into the car.

A few hundred yards later he said, 'Stop now, this is where I want to get off.' Around the car was nothing but open countryside. The old man climbed out of the car with his white poodle. I felt less than happy at leaving him there, because it was a bitterly cold December morning. I was amazed at the accuracy of his directions, as I drew to a halt outside the district nurse's house.

Her welcome was warm and the party well attended. My pains had gone and it turned out to be about the best party I had ever had. I knew that Satan had not wanted me to go to it.

As I was leaving I told the people at the party about the little old man. They asked me to describe him. I went into detail about his weather beaten appearance and the white poodle.

One of the ladies said, 'That must have been an angel sent to guide you. There is no one of that description in the village.' I left the house not really thinking about it and began to make my way back into the village so that I could reach the main road going towards Swindon.

The spot in the open countryside where I had dropped the white-haired old man and his poodle wasn't empty. It had been five hours since I had gone into the house, but the man and the poodle were standing on the same spot as I had left them. An angel is God's messenger and that man definitely seemed to have been like an angel. To this day, I am convinced that I met an angel of God. Normally I would never have asked anyone who was a stranger to get into the car with me, but with that man I felt no fear.

It was one of the most wonderful experiences I had had through doing the parties.

10   *Chosen by God*

George's story...

When Sue got back from Berlin I wanted to escape to
the bathroom to avoid her constant chatter about the
Jews. My father had hated the Jews. I remembered
him saying, 'They are a money-grabbing race who
only help themselves.'

I never had contact with any and was indifferent to
them. The gift of a car to Sue showed me the Lord's
seal on her ministry and led me to pray for her
parties, but I avoided any contact with Israeli
Products Centre.

Sue wanted me to support her when she went for
her first party. I prayed and asked, 'Lord, help me to
fit in. I'm not interested in the Jews and I don't want
it to be a waste of time going.' Only a few friends and
neighbours were there when we arrived. Sue
displayed the jewellery and various goods on a table
rather like a Tupperware party. She was feeling
nervous and I smiled reassuringly at her. She read a
short talk about the inventions achieved by Jews and
God's purposes for Israel. My mind wandered and,
noticing a dark-haired lady next to me looking very

unhappy, I resolved to talk to her. When Sue was released from the strain of having to speak in public at her first party, and began laughing and joking and mixing with the guests who were mainly housewives, the dark-haired lady turned hesitantly towards me. We introduced ourselves.

'I'm George, you're not looking too happy, can I be of any help?' sympathetically I encouraged her to share her fears.

'Yes, my life is a mess and I do need someone to talk to. I don't know why I came tonight,' she said.

'I do, it's so you can share with me,' I finished for her. The rest of the evening took on a significant meaning for me as God fitted me into the party. Still I had very little interest in the Jews. After that it became a pattern for any parties that I attended to find at least one person wanting to share problems and difficulties.

One night Carol came to babysit. My reserve with her was slowly thawing but had not completely gone. Sue enthusiastically and uninhibitedly launched into an account of just what the Lord was showing her about the need for Christian involvement in her work and some of her experiences at Israeli parties. My attention wandered and my eyes looked away from Carol and Sue, sitting side by side.

I lost track of the conversation returning to it as Carol was speaking, 'It's good the Lord has given you something to focus your attention on, Sue, it will do you good.' Carol remarked glancing at my disinterested face. I expect she began praying for me. Sue already was!

During those first few parties, I was forced to hear regularly Sue speaking of the Christian responsibility to the Jews.

She would say, 'We are asked by the Lord in the Bible to pray for the peace of Jerusalem.' At home she expanded often on what the Lord had done for her that day. I passed through uncertainty into puzzlement and finally the desire to pray about my own response. It all took a long period of time.

Sylvia managed to have a party at the manse, but her teenage daughter, Cathleen, missed it and rang up to get an invitation to see for herself the products. Cathleen turned up on an evening when I was busy. Sue pulled the old suitcase off the top of the wardrobe and struggled downstairs with it to the front room. Cathleen helped Sue as she spread it over the patterned living-room carpet. The goods covered the floor area and they knelt together between them. Sue began telling Cathleen where in Israel the items had come from.

'This green stone in the necklace is an Elat Stone and it is made from materials found in King Solomon's mines.' Sue paused and looked up as I entered through the door and cautiously surveyed the scene. She then turned towards Cathleen and carried on chatting.

I stepped warily between the products until I reached the armchair in which I wanted to sit. As no one took any interest in me I looked down and the quality of the products struck me with surprise. I picked one cup up and twisted it in my hand to have a closer look. I placed it carefully down from where I had got it and took up a children's wooden toy and began examining it.

'This is the first time, Sue, that I've really looked at what you're selling. The quality is great,' I remarked to them both, 'Everything is just right.'

'I'm not likely to sell it if it is no good!' Sue retorted indignantly.

'Sorry, love, I didn't mean it like that,' I said with a grin.

At the party I had been to with Sue I had been amazed at the quiet authority with which she spoke. The confidence she had in her subject must have given her that and her burden seemed constantly in different ways to be reconfirmed. My own prayers for her personally must have helped but now I wanted to pray for myself.

Sincerely and expectantly I spoke with God that evening: 'Lord if you want me to be involved with the Jews I want my burden to match Sue's.' Love gradually poured into me for the Jews and I developed an awareness that Jesus was the Messiah of Israel. The cross was not there just because the Jews rejected God, for the Romans actually nailed Him there and pierced His side to ensure He was dead. At Jesus' death, the heathen and the chosen race took equal parts. The world God loved, and guilty men, were mingled for God loved His enemies. We had all managed to be that before coming to Jesus!

My burden became real and together with Sue I was able to start to do the work God had given us. A burning desire to visit the Holy Land began and a coach tour of Christians from a church in the Swindon area gave us the opportunity.

The Lord provided and soon we were gazing out over the Lake of Galilee where Jesus met with His disciples, visiting the birthplace of Jesus and the garden tomb.

Our guide was a Jewish girl called Naomi. She spoke movingly and sincerely. The Lord had spoken to me before the tour. 'George, I want you to take your tithe with you and I will show you the person to give it too.' Of course I prayed on the trip that the Lord would show me who it was for. It would seem logical for it to have been a Christian. At the end of the tour I felt an inner prompting to go to the Jewish guide and offer it to her.

A little red in the face and uncomfortably I went up to her at the front of the bus, 'God wants you to have this money,' I said pushing it quickly into her hand and hoping no one had seen me. She spoke in a cultured English voice and smiled at me.

'Thank you very much, it is very kind of you.' Sue and I were able to talk and share with Naomi and get to know her better, before stepping on the plane back to England. She agreed to come and visit us in our home.

Seemingly unrelated to our interest in the Jewish people, Sue and I, as we were going to Israel for the first time, had contemplated moving to a bigger house. Arriving back from the tour, we began in earnest to look for a property suitable for our growing children, one of whom had nearly reached his coming-of-age party. It was natural for us to pray, 'God bless us, this house and use it in some way to do with the Jews.'

House hunting was the gruelling exercise of trekking around estate agents and armed with papers chasing houses that had already gone. Our own house didn't sell.

One evening I felt the Lord say to me, 'George, do you not trust me to provide for you?'

'Yes, I do Lord,' I said confidently.

'You don't have to get the maximum price for the house, I will make it up for you. I want you to drop it by £1000,' the inner voice prompted me.

I was a bit dismayed but reluctantly said, 'O.K., Lord you win.' The next morning the price was reduced and a young couple came, and as I told them the sum we had just set, the relief showed on their faces.

'That is all we could afford,' the young man said, 'We can have it.' We had sold the house but had nowhere to live!

At another estate agents we were handed the details of a very expensive house and we were nearly put off by the price but went up to see it more out of curiosity.

The split-level house looked like a palatial mansion after our small house. The garden sloped down, to end at a stream, which ran the entire length of the bottom of the garden. The empty house gave even more of an impression of space. Sue stood in the utility room off the kitchen. A trap door was fixed in the floor.

She started to pray, 'Lord, we don't know if this is the house you want us to have but if it is please show it clearly to us.' Sue was silently praying when she had a vision or picture flash across her mind. She was looking at the post of the front wrought-iron gate and by the side of it was the garden wall. On that wall was a sign. It read, 'Emmanuel'. Then she saw the trap door and underneath it Jews were hidden. Pictures of men in authority chasing them came into her thinking. As quickly as it came, it went and, excited, she related to me what she had seen.

'Despite the expense, Sue, I think we've found the house to be happy in and if God wants us to use it to help the Jews He will confirm it,' I told her.

'Let's try putting in an offer. If they accept it, we will know definitely it's the place for us,' Sue said as we left. Our offer was accepted and we were preparing to move when we learnt about the situation of Russian Jews and the vision that Christians had in Europe to prepare for a mass exodus of Jews from the Soviet Union. Listening to tapes and reading *Exodus 11* increased our assurance that God was wanting us to prepare also. We, too, were to use what we had to help Jews who would be among those leaving. The men in authority Sue had seen in her vision were the Russian authorities who didn't want the Jews to leave. Our house would take in Jews in every available space. At that time we were not aware that under the trap door was a space which covered a large area and was the height of an ordinary room.

Naomi came over to visit us a couple of weeks before we were moving in and we were able to show her the house. We learnt much more about her. She was an atheist but proud of her Jewish ancestry. She had read the Bible, studied the Koran, examined Buddhist philosophy and absorbed the essence of Hindu mysticism. On all those subjects she spoke with authority, although she could not accept that Jesus had been born of a virgin. Our friendship grew, however, and before she went back to Israel she invited us to stay with her family in the heart of her homeland. We made plans to go the following year at Easter.

Less than a week after moving into our new house we discovered our next-door neighbours were Jews. For us it was the seal of approval on our move, and we had to wait and see what God wanted to do with us and what we had in the future.

Sue carried on with her parties and even had one to which people from the village came. I drove Sue over to another party shortly afterwards, it was another one in Stroud. As Sue was speaking I knew there was someone in the room, a lady, suffering from stomach pains.

So I said out aloud, 'There's a lady here with very bad stomach pains which the Lord wants to heal.' All around me there was an embarrassed silence. I had never done that before. As there was no answer someone suggested that the group should sing. They sang a chorus but as they were singing again I knew I had to speak.

So I repeated: 'There's someone here with stomach pains and the Lord wants to heal you.'

This time a lady spoke with a quiet voice, 'That person is me. The first time I wasn't sure it could be me and so I asked the Lord that if it was me the message would be repeated a second time.' She came forward and hands were laid on her for healing. God answered. The lady would not have been blessed if I had been too concerned with my embarrassment or refused to obey the Lord.

Obedience is a lifelong commitment and in my own case needs constantly reaffirming. In the order of my Christian priorities, uppermost in my mind was the need to evangelise: reaching out to others so that God can change their lives and forgive their sins. Many in the churches were, in my eyes, overlooking people. They were, by their lack of reaching out, blocking people off from the sight of God. Some were even unapproachable.

A lady on a bus trip to hear Billy Graham, when he was in Bristol, came from Wales. She said that all the people on the bus were good Welsh church folk and they hadn't brought one non-believer with them. That is what I really mean by unapproachable. I believe a broader outlook is achieved only as prayer becomes an important part of our lives. It has become a lifeline of communication for me.

Being a Christian at work in a secular and tough environment has kept me in touch with reality. People there blame God for world catastrophes and give God no credit for making men and women. They use His name only in abuse of one another. As a Christian I am aware of the scrutiny and criticism present but often when they are in trouble they want my help.

In the canteen once I overheard a man talking with the woman behind the counter. She was passing sympathetic remarks to him. I gathered his niece had just been given a few weeks to live. The man walked away with his cup when the woman gave her attention to me.

'Don't you think you ought to do something for him,' she said, knowing my Christian beliefs.

'Yes, I think you're right, I'll go and get him,' hurriedly I followed the worker whom I didn't know very well.

Sitting around a table it wasn't long before I was telling him how Sue was healed and that Jesus could not only help but heal.

'Jesus can choose to heal Amanda,' I said.

Her uncle explained, 'They think Amanda has

leukaemia and she has cancer of the kidneys.'

Amanda was still a child and a real pity overwhelmed me for the suffering she was going through. Soon I was meeting Amanda's parents and Reg and Sylvia also prayed with them. As we prayed together, the Lord spoke to me.

'Take the little girl's hand as you pray, George.' I reached over and took her wasted hand. The parents came along to church and God was obviously trying to comfort them. She was pale but happy. Amanda for a while got better, a few weeks came and went and she seemed to be progressing. She even went back to school. But it was not to last. She was rushed into hospital and one cancerous kidney was removed but the other one was badly damaged. The threat of leukaemia still hung over her.

The specialist said, 'She has only a 10% chance of living.' Others joined us in prayer for this small child. It looked hopeless and the whole situation was distressing for the parents and relatives and those of us who had got to know Amanda. Christians from our church joined together to pray for her. The blood results came back and we heard the news that Amanda had not got leukaemia after all. We had something in the tragedy to praise the Lord for! Her chances of living were increasing. We do not know yet whether she will live but we see that through prayer the parents are given the grace to cope and much comfort and support. God is wanting us to see Him as a God of comfort.

A director I knew came to me in great distress one day.

'George,' he said anxiously, 'My daughter has

been in a car crash and is in the intensive care unit at the hospital. Will you come and pray for her?'

I was learning something new. When doctors give a patient a 50% chance of living, people try praying, thinking it helps tip the scales towards healing. If the patient recovers, they probably attribute it to medical science rather than divine help. But if the doctors fail and every possible avenue of help has been explored in detail, then they turn to prayer in desperation. Their total reliance is on prayer and the hope that God will hear and answer them.

I went into this small crowded intensive care unit with all its complicated technical equipment and prayed and asked the Lord to heal her injuries. I went out, uncertain that God had answered, but feeling I had given the only real help to that family I could. Within two weeks the girl went home completely healed. A miracle had happened!

The lady in the works canteen asked me to pray for a girl with a brain tumour and she told me the surname of the parents. I was about to set off on a journey to Carteton and loaded up my gear and set off in the van. Driving along keeping my eyes on the road, I began singing in tongues. After singing I experienced an urgency to contact these parents. It was so urgent that I stopped at the nearest telephone booth and flipped through a directory. The page fell open at the surname: there was a number with the same name.

An inner voice spoke, 'That's the one you need.' I had no other way of knowing, as I didn't know his first name. The father answered the phone, and carefully I explained why I was phoning. He asked me to come round and visit him and his wife.

Sue came with me and I asked them, 'Would you like me to pray for Lisa?'

Her Dad replied, 'No' we don't want to upset her; we would rather you didn't. Thank you for your help.' Lisa we knew had been given only two weeks to live but to look at her it was incredible. She was a bouncy child with colour in her cheeks. It was hard to believe she was dying from an inoperable tumour, but not for long. A week later the difference was astounding, she had gone rapidly downhill. The parents asked us to pray and we did, but Sue could not get any assurance that she would be healed. When we went round to Lisa's parents' home, Lisa had been in a coma for three days. Her fair hair never left the pillow as we came in and she was in a half coma. She was ten years old. She died shortly afterwards and we rang up and the mother answered.

She told me, 'Lisa was at peace when she died and she passed away without any pain.' The parents asked Reg, our pastor, to take the funeral service. Reg brought a message of comfort to the parents. In that instance only through the strength of prayer could acceptance of what had happened be achieved. Lisa's parents came along to the fellowship and people showed them loving concern. God had guided me to them and the purpose He intended for me in the meeting of that family was to show them that He was a loving, concerned God. He was the one who comforts, as the word of God states, 'Blessed are those who mourn for they shall be comforted' (Matthew 5:4).

That God wants to heal, I am sure, but equally certain am I, that healing for some may only come when they reach His presence. God has done so much for me and I am grateful that I can praise Him. The only thing I can give Him is my life. I must take up the cross in my daily life. I must face suffering and help others who suffer. I am not superhuman and my constant mistakes are painful to me. The advantage given to me is to know that the God who met me didn't bump me off because I failed Him. He forgave me, released me, and gave me a new life. Heaven here I come!

11 *The desert shall blossom*

Sue's story...

My stomach was constricted and my throat was dry and parched as the music began. George never even glanced in my direction, let alone showed any awareness of my problem. The impulse to get out overcame me. Sweating, I steeled myself to listen to the message, join in the choruses and hymns and to sit wedged between the crowd about me of men, women and children. It was getting worse! 'You stupid woman, control yourself,' I told myself sternly. A sensation of panic swept over me as I was thinking. It was the same feeling that I had had when preparing for church, but which I had quelled as we got in the car. I wondered if I had really wanted to come as much as I thought I did. My subconscious mind must be playing havoc in me.

A nightmare of fear was descending into my well-ordered, contented life. The fear crept in slowly until it paralysed me in church. My hands and feet would sweat until they were wet and the miserable thing was I couldn't explain what was happening to myself or to others. Panic sprung out of the fear but came on gradually and in degrees. Worst of all, it plagued me in church meetings and spoiled everything. Alone, I could pray a bit, but in a worship service I was becoming more and more aware of the fact that I was scared. My friends were all there, but it made no difference: over the two or three months I just couldn't cope.

Life was still relatively normal, and nowhere else did I feel my sensations: once out of the church building they disappeared as if they hadn't happened. It was so foolish I hid it from George. I made excuses not to attend the services.

'George, I will have to stay and cook this meal, it needs watching.' 'I meant to do this in the week, I'm afraid I must get it done now.'

'Are you sure, Sue, you always seem to be missing services?' George questioned one morning.

But out of my feeling of embarrassment and because I thought I was being a hysterical woman, the moment passed for me to tell him. I suffered alone. There were problems at the time within the church and my absence passed without comment. During the week I had Christian fellowship with a few friends.

Getting into my car after packing it for an Israeli party, suddenly the sweating began again and I shook, steeling myself and praying. The Lord must have driven my car there. I arrived back home, but now I was facing panic anywhere. It was an endurance test next day to go into town for my shopping. Again my stomach churned over and a feeling of nausea invaded me. Coping with ordinary everyday life as well as the church was the latest problem! I had made excuses about church but now needed to make excuses not to go to other places. A trip out to see my friend Margaret for a shopping trip was an ordeal by fire. In a crowd I broke out in a sweat and my tongue cleaved to the roof of my mouth. Confused that a perfectly sane, rather brusque yet often happy person could become in a matter of three months a nervous and physical wreck drove me to visit the doctor.

'I don't want tranquillisers, I've just heard they're no good for you,' I said, sitting uncomfortably in the seat, wringing my hands.

'You do seem to need a little help for a while. Tranquillisers for a very short time do not become addictive, I can assure you,' he replied, scribbling out a prescription. A feeling of alarm came over me but I was too tired to argue.

The Valium I picked up at the chemist and took home seemed no answer to me. It never got taken, I tried to live with my symptoms as they got worse. The housegroup and George eventually realised that I was not myself and prayed for me. The cloud did not lift from me. Sympathetically, people sought to help me cope. I sat near the door in meetings so I could escape outside into the fresh air and open space. My friends helped and encouraged me with shopping.

I froze with fright when I heard of a housegroup outing to see *Dick Whittington*. George was firm that I should go along.

'You can't expect me to be in that mass of people and all that noise,' I wailed.

'If you stop going to pleasure trips, Sue, you've given up. You're going,' George said finally.

Miserable and depressed, and my stomach doing

cartwheels and my mouth like a desert, I arrived at the pantomime with the whole family. The lobby was already filled with waiting theatre-goers. Members of the housegroup were standing near the glass doors. Margaret handed me my ticket and while we waited I edged close to the entrance onto the balcony trying to imagine I wasn't there, as panic assailed me.

That evening passed for me in a haze, I sat at the back on the edge of a row. The performance was hilarious but I couldn't laugh. I waited impatiently to get outside.

For a year my illness got worse as I walked out of the front door but was better as I arrived back in my own home. George tried to cheer me up and booked a Christmas holiday for us all in the Canary Islands. It was to be at the paradise resort of Lanzarote. On the plane journey I sat as close to the toilet as I could, screwed my eyes shut and clasped my hands. My teeth ground together in determination not to make a scene. After a year of my symptoms there was nothing I could do which would stop a reaction.

We arrived in brilliant sunshine and pulled our summer clothes from the suitcases. In thin cotton we walked everywhere. George and the kids were eager to reach the beach, I followed behind reasonably calm, enjoying the heat of the sun's rays on my arms. The beach was just starting to swarm with holiday-makers as we arrived, wearing our sunglasses and ready for a day in the fresh air.

The sea was a Mediterranean blue, I breathed in the salty smell and wriggled my toes in the sand. The children stripped off and put on their swim wear. As the morning wore on and the sun got hotter I turned over onto my back and looked around me. People were closing in on me on all sides. Striped deckchairs, buckets, spades and baskets were littered everywhere.

'No, no,' I thought, 'it can't be'. I felt I was being squeezed inwards. Someone was placing me in a tin can and sealing on the lid. On an open beach with a calm and beautiful tropical paradise, the nightmare flared again. Agony and pain ran through my mind. Familiar blinding panic seized me and held on. Hurriedly and without really knowing what I was doing, I got to my feet. I grabbed my clothes and pushed them onto my tense body. My muscles were hard and knotted. No question of coping entered my mind as I was so overwhelmed. It was as if I was drowning in my fear.

'What on earth are you doing?' George remarked looking up at me with startled eyes, which were screwed up to shield them from the glare of the sun.

'It's no good. I've got to get away from here. Leave me alone! I'll be all right later!' I moaned. 'You don't understand, I just can't cope. I'm sorry.' Stumbling slightly and trying to move away I turned, looking towards the distant holiday hotels which were pure white in the sunshine. George grabbed hold of my damp and trembling hand and convulsively my grip tightened as I sought support and comfort.

'Sue, if you go, we all go. Wait while I call the kids.' He yelled and they came running. Disappointed and subdued, they left the beach. Guilty, confused and unhappy it seemed I couldn't even pray. God didn't seem there in that situation! 'When we get back home Sue, you're going to have some ministry about this. It can't go on.' George said on our return to the villa. He was adamant. Wretchedly, but not keen on the idea, I agreed.

'O.K. I'll ask for help but I've prayed about it before. Perhaps I'm meant to suffer it or maybe it will go away as suddenly as it came,' I said as we went to bed. The remainder of the holiday we avoided the beach and crowded places. My panic ruined everyone's enjoyment, and feeling guilty didn't alleviate it at all.

The incident on the beach was the final straw, but one other happening made me face reality. My brother Tony died and George and I went to attend his funeral. We were griefstricken. To make matters worse, the day before the funeral George had received a nasty blow on the head at work. So despite my fears, I had to drive the car on the long journey to the church. It was like a dream, I shed silent tears as I reached the wooden pew before the service began. There was no way that I would miss Tony's funeral for he was my beloved brother. Strangled almost with the turbulence of my emotions I reached for the hymn book. As the service went on, everything intensified until I thought I would scream, but respect and love for my brother kept me until the bitter end. Grief did not overcome my panic. For nothing in the world would I have missed Tony's funeral but still I experienced the same peculiar sensations.

In the New Year, Margaret urged me to see Reg and Sylvia and they made an appointment for me to come for prayer counselling. Tingles ran down my back as I sat in my bath on the arranged morning. Getting into my car to drive to the manse I needed the Lord's hands to steady me. A quivering wreck, I began the short trip. My praying was not free and I found no release from my fears. I gave up the attempt, as weariness engulfed me. I drove slowly reflecting whether to turn back or not. Arriving late at the manse, they must have been wondering whether I was coming!

Gently Reg spoke and reassured me as I sank into a chair. He probed, 'How are you feeling, Sue?'

'I feel terrible, it's all these flashes of panic. My stomach churns, my throat is parched, my hands and feet sweat, I can't cope, I feel so much fear.'

Once I started to share, it was easy to confide in them as friends. When they prayed, peace came flooding into me and dissolved the iron bands of fear which I had feebly tried myself to release. The more we prayed together, the more liberty I gained. At the end of that long session, relaxed, my muscles limp, I sat comfortable in the chair. Once again prayer flowed and I knew from then on I could cope. There would be times of anxiety and stress but never would I lose myself in it. God had helped me through the suffering, but my experience was not without value. Because of that experience my understanding of the needs of people in distress was accentuated. Shut off for a while from God, the return of peace was much more precious to me and I took it less for granted. It was a lesson to learn that Christians have their problems but their source of help never fails. God continues to be concerned and to guide us, giving us a full life.

Our second trip to Israel was a great joy. Burning with love for the Jews, I was longing to see Israel again. For the first time we were to stay with a Jewish family. As Christians we were celebrating Easter, but for our Jewish friends it was the time of the Passover. Naomi's Jewish family accepted us and we stayed in a three-bedroomed luxury apartment in Jerusalem. Some of the family practised the Jewish religious rites as well as the cultural obligations of their race. When Naomi's mother served us with milk in the coffee after eating meat, it was a great sacrifice which we all appreciated. She never mixed milk with meat! Some Jews followed the laws of the Sabbath rigidly and others ignored them, but all were conscious of their Jewish inheritance.

Just before we arrived in Jerusalem a bus was hijacked, so the evidence of unrest was all around. The unity of the Jewish family and relatives was impressive and we were really touched when they invited us to share the Passover with them. The strangers in their midst were welcomed in. No reference was made to our Christian faith, but we had already learnt that Jews divide the known world into two categories, either Muslim or Christian. It is a horrifying thought that it is possible for them to believe that Hitler's holocaust perpetrators were Christians. It is not just barriers of doctrine that separate the Jews from the Gentiles. We were left feeling we had to show only the love of Jesus through our lives; our words would never be enough. As Christians we hoped our lives wouldn't be too much of a failure in that situation. We regretted our weaknesses and hoped we wouldn't let the Lord down.

For the Passover we sat around with our hostess's mother and brother, two other brothers and their wives and Naomi and her two teenage children. It was a solemn occasion and we ate the kosher food.

The bread was unleavened to show stealth and the speed with which the people fled from Egypt to escape Pharoah. There were exotic salads to eat with it and delicious cakes from the unleavened flour again. Readings from the Haggadah told the familiar story we knew. We were grateful to be there and to know that God was still guiding us today. He didn't just lead His chosen people from Egypt, but all of us chosen by God can experience His guidance anytime.

At the end of our holiday we went on a cold and beautiful day and we climbed up the Mount of Olives. For us it was a place with a special atmosphere. Tranquil and peaceful, it was a memory to take back with us as we left Jerusalem and our family behind.

I had booked an Israeli party on my return, but there I encountered some opposition.

A large lady kept on interrupting my talk, 'Why bother to help the Jews?' she said belligerently, while I was speaking of the inflation in Israel today.

Because of the other wives there, I ignored her and carried on talking, after pausing to say, 'My talk will explain that.' She was oblivious of anybody else there; it was as if she was the only person at the party. As she kept on interrupting, I grew angry and annoyed but began to display the items I had brought. I lifted up in my left hand a blue tie with the Star of David pattern on it, and the large lady looked disgusted. I hesitated.

She spoke in a high-pitched voice, 'Look at that hideous star plastered all over that tie.'

It was with a real effort of willpower I said in a controlled way, 'Well, don't buy the tie, then.' I fixed my attention on the other nine women gathered and raced through the other items not daring to stop in case she spoke. I finished breathless but relieved. 'Just come and see what you would like. Each of you should have an order sheet from Israeli Products Centre.' I smiled at them while thinking perhaps I should have been more patient with the only non-Christian present. I prayed quickly, 'Lord forgive me.'

Soon after that I was praying again! The large dissatisfied woman picked up a number of items and also a copy of *Selected to Live*. She was lingering indecisively so I said rather curtly, 'I should read that. It will do you a power of good!' She decided to have a copy and I flushed guiltily wishing I had been less nasty.

There was more opposition to our work and George and I were called 'do-gooders', 'holier than thou', and 'Jew lovers', but the certainty that we were following the plan the Lord had for us in our life helped us to press on to help Christians to reach out to Jews. George and I were united in this which was a blessing through our many struggles.

A newspaper cutting about an organisation helping Jewish people to leave Russia led to our personal involvement praying and writing to Jews who were trying to get exit visas to leave Russia to return to Israel. It was a further step when we also made contact with a Russian prisoner. From these beginnings the Lord is still leading us as now we are forming a local committee to help Russian Jews seeking release from the Soviet Union.

God has given us a ministry but we have also been involved with the people.

Some things bring the past back to you and Josie's telephone call did that for me.

'Hi, Sue, long time no see! I heard that you went to a faith-healer.' Josie's cheerful Irish brogue vibrated across the wires.

'Josie, lovely to hear you. It wasn't a faith-healer, Jesus helped me,' I warmly greeted her. A picture of her tall, graceful form came into my mind. There was an uncomfortable long silence and a discreet cough told me Josie's reactions. Hoping she wouldn't ring off I hurried to speak. 'Josie, come up and see me and have a chat for old times sake!'

We had met when I had not long had Tony. Josie had come from County Down as a pregnant sixteen-year-old. She had hid it from her father until she was eight and half months pregnant. Shunted off to a convent and then into families with a small baby, she had just come back home as an unmarried mother to the stares of her neighbours. On the way along she dropped her Catholic faith and turned atheist. Josie became my friend on my 21st birthday. Her accent made her difficult to understand, but her sense of humour was hard to resist. We laughed and swore together. Josie married a policeman and had two more children but we kept in touch. She had a natural talent for singing and as a professional singer she toured the pubs and working men's clubs. George and I would go to one of her 'gigs' just to support her. When I fell ill with cancer she had realised it was serious when the doctor had diagnosed wind. While unconscious after my operation she had sat with me, distressed and disturbed about the fragility of life. George and she ended that evening together in the pub drinking until closing time. Soon after, Josie and her husband split up and divorced and we lost touch.

Josie came over one morning to see and explained that my name had appeared in a local newspaper. The article told how I had been healed from cancer. Josie's eldest daughter had a rare eye disease which had caused benign tumours to grow. Anna was so distressed that she needed help.

'Jesus can help you if you let him. George and I are different people,' I said enthusiastically. Josie noticed that, George's and my eyes looked very different, my every other word wasn't a swear word and somehow my youth had returned to me. To Josie I looked younger than the last time she saw me. 'Come along to a Full Gospel Business Men's Dinner. Here's an invite,' I said pushing two tickets into her hand.

'I am not sure Sue. It's very interesting but don't you think you have gone a bit overboard on this religion lark?' her anxiety showed through her voice.

'You'll see for yourself. God can help you too.' It was exciting to share again.

Reluctantly Josie and her daughter came along to the Monday evening dinner.

Josie was horrified, 'Look here Sue, there's no smoking, and water in the glasses.'

I didn't know why she was worried as she had come along drunk and high on cannabis anyway. George and I prayed for them. Josie hated the meeting but at the end she went forward looking for help for her own problems as well as her daughter's. George and I went with them.

The speaker said, 'Have you taken Jesus as your own personal Saviour?'

Josie, red with embarrassment, and flustered mumbled, 'Yes' without conviction.

The car journey back was a silent one. I was quick to arrange to see more of her. Josie became very guilty that as a once Catholic she should have anything to do with us. Why she agreed to come to another dinner I don't know, but she did. Her guitarist partner came too. At the meeting people sang in tongues and both of them were standing open-mouthed.

'That's just amazing, Sue, I've never heard music so beautiful and harmonious.' As they sang professionally, the quality amazed them. Josie's interest faded during the rest of the evening and the guitarist she brought along walked out. The tug of loyalty for us only kept Josie in her seat though she moved about restlessly.

Anger blazed in her face and she got up at the closing prayer and strode towards the men waiting to minister.

'What do you mean about this personal Saviour business?' she demanded recklessly.

One of them interrupted her, 'Are you a Roman Catholic?'

She exploded, 'What if I am?'

'Come with me and talk with the Catholic priest here. He'll help you,' the man said, gently steering her back towards where George and I were sitting. Father O'Ryan was next to us so she sat down heavily.

With her usual wry humour she remarked, 'What do you think the Pope thinks about all this?' Father O'Ryan laughed and kept on trying to reassure her. We talked of faith and God's help. Josie, her life messed up and addicted to cannabis, was rebellious.

'The cannabis never harms me,' she said to reassure herself more than us. But taking cannabis had opened her up so that she was attracted to occult practices. Her skill with the *I Ching* had made her popular with friends. Astrology was her hobby. 'I can see people have something I haven't, like you and George, but I can't get it myself,' she said wistfully but defiantly, 'I've been reading my Bible but it doesn't make sense.'

We prayed for her release and George went round to her house to pray for her eldest daughter's eyes. Anna awoke the next morning with clearer eyes. Josie was wrestling with frustration and confusion and so we prayed to comfort her.

Later she renounced her contact with the occult. Easily then she destroyed the dice and other things connected with *I Ching*. Josie read more of her Bible and sought to find God.

On a Wednesday morning, three months after we had met again, she awoke knowing she had been 'born again' and had met with God. The Bible now held a new meaning for her. Within three weeks she was leading others to Jesus!

I didn't look for God, but He came to me. He changed a swearing, godless, selfish and hard woman in a moment in time to a cleansed, accepted one. Cancer was nothing to Him. George's alcoholism was even cured by the touch of the living God. In two people He has performed miracles and gives us rich and full lives. I know God can take anyone and give them hope.

God is waiting to write your name in His book or maybe it is already there along with mine. If you've read this book you know we were saved from the scrap heap and built into the Body of Christ. Two rough diamonds added to the crown of God!

Other titles published by
TORBAY PUBLISHING

'This Do Ye', Roy Peacock
Light in Your Darkness, Harry Greenwood
The Diakonate, Dale Rumble
Beyond the ash pit, Michael Darwood
The words that I speak, John Hutchison
Miracle In The Mirror, Nita Edwards
   and Mark Buntain
Christ's Healing Ministry Today, Michael Darwood
Christian Counselling, Ron Smith

New releases 1984

Live Like a King, Don Double
The Tug of Two Loves, Meg Scott
Divorced but not Defeated, Meg Scott
Reclaimed!, Helen Penfold